for Lyn
(man
Marlena

# Body-Centered Coaching

## Marlena Field

**Foreword by Donna Martin**

BODY MIND SPIRIT
Victoria, British Columbia

Copyright © 2005 Marlena Field

All rights reserved. No part of this publication may be reproduced, transmitted in any form or by any means, electronic, mechanical, photocopying, recording, or otherwise, without the prior written consent of the publisher, except in the case of brief quotations embedded in critical articles and reviews, with credit given to the author.

**Library and Archives Canada Cataloguing in Publication**

Field, Marlena, 1947-
Body-centered coaching / Marlena Field.

Includes bibliographical references.
ISBN 0-9736643-3-9

1. Mentoring.  2. Mind and body.  3. Motivation (Psychology)
4. Success–Psychological aspects.  I. Title.

RZ400.F53 2005  158'.3  C2005-901974-3

**Cover and Layout**
Kelly Hewkin, IntuitiveGraphicDesign.com

**Published by Body Mind Spirit**
**Victoria, British Columbia**

Printed in Canada

To my dear friend

**Eleanor Hanrahan**

we have shared our love of books
for almost forty years

# Contents

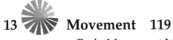

ACKNOWLEDGEMENTS

# Acknowledgements

I would not have begun this book without the love, encouragement and generous contribution from my dear friend Donna Martin. Her belief in me and the body-centered approach to working with clients has been a huge support.

I was blessed with my 'family of editors'. My appreciation to:

> My husband Jim: for his commitment of time and energy to this project. He offered me love, encouragement and devotion beyond belief. Without his input this book would not be as well written. Happily, we were an exception to the rule – never have a spouse edit your book. We have a great relationship and a joint interest in my subject.

> My daughter Meghan: for her generosity in reading through the manuscript and offering concrete and insightful suggestions. Her belief in me and her pride in my work are heart-warming.

My son Jeremy: for his feedback about what he felt was the heart of my book. It's an unbelievable experience to hear, "Meghan and I are really proud of you, Mom."

My sister Shirley: for her proof-reading and specific feedback. It was wonderful to have another pair of loving eyes reading my book.

My friend Kathy McCabe: for her proof-reading and careful attention to detail.

I was also blessed with colleagues and friends who were willing to read my book and write testimonials. Thanks to Sherry LeBlanc, Steve Mitten, Arnold Porter, Val Sharp and Jan Sommer.

I also want to acknowledge the encouragement and support that I felt from Sue Bond, Suzan Bond, Paula Beltgens, Linda Clark, Mary Eshenko, Beth Falch-Neilsen, Carlin Favell, Lowell Ann Fulsang, the Black Goddesses, Ully Graf, David Greenshields, Eleanor Hanrahan, Peggy Hansen, Charon Hunniford, Carolyn Hutchinson, George Johnson, Pamela Lewis, Michael Lines, Joanne McLean, Julia Menard, Ardis Myette, Debbie Nikkel, Valerie Owen, Mike Ray, Thea Sheldon, Jessie Sutherland, Elsbeth Tate, Brian Walsh, Terrill Welch and Anita Wolfe. And of course, my wonderful clients, many of whom are disguised in the client stories.

Working with Kelly Hewkin, of Intuitive Graphic Design, on the book cover design and the formatting was a joy. I could count on her creativity, expertise, attention to detail and sense of humor every step of the way.

# Foreword

This is the kind of book I love: at once readable and profound, inspiring and practical, informative and accessible.

Marlena Field and I have been friends for almost thirty years. When I say that she has put her heart into this book, as she does with everything, it is with a huge appreciation for her whole-hearted approach to life, her warmth, her joy, her spirit, her love of helping others, and her contagious enthusiasm. I think it comes through clearly in this delightful book.

I feel confident that you will pick up the spirit of that as you read it, along with all the tips and techniques that make this "body-centered" approach to working so effective.

Marlena and I started training in the Hakomi Method of Body-Centered Psychotherapy together in 1990. I have gone on to become a trainer in that method, while Marlena has developed her skills as a personal and professional coach. Both of us have felt and witnessed the profound affect of paying attention to the wisdom of the body in our own lives and in working with others.

I am thrilled to see her take the essence of the body-mind-spirit approach, adapt it to the coaching situation, and create in this book a simple yet powerfully effective tool for others to use in their work and in their lives.

I think this book will help anyone working with others in a "client-centered" way to access deeper levels of intuitive knowing, clarity, peace of mind, confidence, inspiration, and creativity in all they do.

I am certain you will want to read *Body-Centered Coaching* again and again and have it close at hand when you work with others. Mostly, I sincerely hope you will begin to use the simple tools shared in this book to enrich your own lives.

Enjoy!

Donna Martin, MA
Certified Hakomi Therapist and Trainer

# Preface

Writing a book and being an author have never been high on my list of priorities. So, the writing of Body-Centered Coaching happened in spite of myself. It began in conversation with colleagues who were curious about using the body in coaching. My response was, "Hey, I know a lot about that." My lifelong learning has been focused on body-centered approaches – to therapy, to acupressure and to coaching. I had a compelling message and became consumed by my passion to share it with others. The end result, which is a surprise to me at some level, is this offering of my book. I hope you take the ideas and techniques and apply them in your work and enjoy the process.

# Introduction

*Body-Centered Coaching* is for coaches and other helping professionals, such as counselors, therapists, social workers, psychologists, mentors and wellness practitioners.

*Body-Centered Coaching* is a resource that you can use immediately to enhance your present abilities in working with people. It is designed as an adjunct to the work you already do with your clients. *Body-Centered Coaching* demonstrates how you can add simple, yet powerful, body-centered techniques to your repertoire of skills. The practice of body-centered coaching can be done in person or over the telephone. The techniques may be used as a small segment of a session or become the whole session.

The client stories are the heart of the book. They are based directly on the experiences of clients. The stories clearly teach the creative process of body-centered coaching and give you an understanding of the client's experience and the possibilities for use in your own practice. There are a total of fifteen stories, all varied to demonstrate the techniques. Overall, the learning will have you move forward in your own mastery as a coach.

You, the reader, have undergone a variety of trainings and life experiences. Therefore, you will use the ideas in this book in ways that will best suit your unique style of working. You will discover new ways to encourage clients towards action and integration. You will definitely experience some "aha!" moments.

## Using the Body as a Resource for Change

The body is an under-utilized resource for learning and change. The practice of body-centered coaching is based on the premise that the body has a natural intelligence and wisdom that can offer coaches, and consequently their clients, a new depth of learning. It involves being curious and intuitive about the language and signals the body is sending. Interpreting the information and then integrating it opens many more creative pathways for both coaches and clients. You cannot *talk* clients out of their perspective; the change needs to be *experienced* through the body.

> **"On the deepest level, change always involves the body."**
> - Ron Kurtz and Hector Prestera
> - The Body Reveals

In service to your client's learning, you can notice what is happening in your own body as well as intuitively sensing what is happening in theirs. During the course of this book, I will be using the body to better understand feelings, thoughts, perspectives, memories, intentions, intuition – many of the diverse aspects of the human experience.

Your subconscious mind often speaks to you through your body. Your body's wisdom can best be accessed by noticing – being curious about it and respecting that its language is different from cognitive and verbal language. Some expressions that are used to talk about the body's language are "sixth sense", "inner knowing", "gut reaction", "still small voice" and "somatic intelligence".

Have you ever heard people say?

- I trusted my gut and just went for it.
- I knew in my heart it was the right thing to do.
- I had a feeling you'd be calling today.
- The hair on the back of my neck stood on end.
- My stomach knotted up with fear.
- My heart began racing.

Yet we do not always pay attention to our bodies. We may be completely disconnected from the information it's offering us at times.

Do you ever…

- use your body merely as a vehicle to carry you around?
- mistreat your body by being critical of it?
- attempt to 'whip' your body into shape?
- berate your body for being weak or out of control?
- act as an unkind and uncaring partner with your body?
- turn a deaf ear to the signals your body gives you such as "I'm tired. I need to have a rest now."
- forget to ask your body what it wants for nourishment?

Ken Wilber states that *"few of us have lost our minds, but most of us have long ago lost our bodies."* He suggests we ride our body much like someone rides a horse.

> *"I beat it or praise it, I feed and clean and nurse it when necessary. I urge it on without consulting it and I hold it back against its will. When my body-horse is well-behaved I generally ignore it, but when it gets unruly – which is all too often – I pull out the whip to beat it back into reasonable submission."*
>
> *- No Boundary:*
> *Eastern and Western Approaches to Personal Growth*

## *The Process of Embodiment*

The process of embodiment involves embracing body, mind and spirit to become a fully integrated person. The practice of body-centered coaching works with the inter-relationship of the *internal* and the *external*. The *internal* involves having your clients notice their *internal* experience: their body sensations and the signals and messages their body is sending. The *external* expands the internal experience to include *external* body experience in the form of posture, gesture or changes in position. When clients move even slightly, the energy can shift to connect the totality of body, mind and spirit – embracing the inter-relationship of all. By involving the wholeness of the body, there is more data available and the learning becomes more integrated.

## The Inter-relationship of Body, Mind and Spirit

The practice of body-centered coaching recognizes that body, mind and spirit are different aspects of your whole being, like different doorways into the same house. Sometimes your heart wants to go in one direction and your mind in another. When you pay attention to body, mind and spirit equally, you listen with all parts of your being – eyes, ears, heart, soul, body, mind – allowing for all parts to be heard and respected. The individual parts partner with each other for the greatest good – for you, those around you and for the environment. You need to listen to your heart's wisdom, as well as your mind. Although you will be using the body as an avenue for insight and learning, the reality is that you are a whole person.

Embodiment of body, mind and spirit speaks to who you are BEING in the world: what you stand for – your values – your purpose – your passions – how you express yourself creatively – how you maximize your gifts, strengths, talents and creativity – how you express what you intend in each moment.

Who you are BEING as a coach is one of the greatest assets that you bring to your clients through the coaching relationship. You bring the true *spirit* of who you are: the essential, authentic, and unique aspects of you. You bring the part of you that can most effectively relate to others and to the world around you, feeling at ease and connected with your own body, mind and spirit.

By being yourself, you are a model for your clients and an encouragement for them to embody who they are. Being yourself is not about being perfect, however. By being imperfect, you act as a model for your clients to accept themselves as they are.

*"...appreciate your broken branches – as a sign of your uniqueness and perfection: we all have imperfections and ego attachments. Not something to be overcome or transcended, rather understood... appreciated... and accepted."*

*- Charlie Badenhop*
*- Pure Heart, Simple Mind newsletter*

## Being and Doing

As a coach, you have the wonderful opportunity to share in another person's life. Consider for a moment all of your coaching skills – the concepts, ideas and strategies that you have in your coaching toolkit. The integration of all of these is vitally important. **Who you are**, however, is what brings your work alive and allows you to be yourself and be with your clients in a way that is fulfilling for both of you. It is the difference between **doing coaching vs. being a coach**. When *being* is in place, then *doing* can occur in a more meaningful way.

Sometimes people complain that we act as if we are human *doings* rather than human *beings*. This is a misunderstanding of your nature. You are a doer. You are designed to do. However, doing is not the opposite of being; you are a human being who does things. Even resting is something you do: so are thinking, eating, sleeping, reading and playing. It's more a question of:

## Who am I BEING while I am DOING?

As an example of *being while doing,* consider the two ways of walking down the street holding hands with a spouse, a child, or another loved one. You will likely relate to both ways.

One way is the *doing of holding hands.* In this example, you are merely going through the action of holding hands without much consciousness or intent. In fact, you may hardly be aware of holding hands or even of the other person's presence. Your mind is somewhere else and your body is merely going through the motions.

The other way is the *being of holding hands.* In this example, you are being aware of your feelings of love and connectedness with the other person. Perhaps you are feeling grateful about the relationship and you enjoy the experience of holding hands. Physically, you can feel their hand in yours. Your whole being is involved in enjoying the experience.

At any moment, when aware of being present, you are at a choice point. You can instantly switch from the *doing of holding hands* to the *being of holding hands.*

## *Being in the Now*

Being with yourself and with another person involves being in the present moment: *in the now.* When you are in the *now,* your compassion, intuition, curiosity and imagination are more accessible to you. It brings you to your essence. Being in the *now* quiets your mind. It is the ability to be with all that is happening in the moment; it is being conscious and aware of what's going on inside you, with your client, and in the surrounding environment.

*"Through self-observation, more presence comes into your life automatically. The moment you realize you are not present, you are present. Whenever you are able to observe your mind, you are no longer trapped in it. Another factor has come in, something that is not of the mind: the witnessing presence."*

-Eckhart Tolle
- The Power of Now: a Guide to Enlightenment

## *Body-Centered Coaching offers you:*

- fifteen varied client stories to illustrate the practice of body-centered coaching; some are whole sessions and some are parts of sessions.
- the embodiment of body, mind and spirit.
- a series of tools to connect you with your body's wisdom.
- the distinction between empowered and disempowered listening and the resulting impact on both you and your client.
- an effective way to make contact with the storyteller – not the story.
- the power and practice of mindfulness.
- techniques for working with coaching issues such as limiting beliefs, decision-making, handling overwhelming emotions, confusions (con-fusions).
- ways to round out a session: helping clients make a stronger connection with their learning and offering ways to remember the experience.
- the use of visualization, identifying body signals, remembering resources and experimenting with

possibilities as powerful ways to move your clients forward.

- the use of key words and language skills for greater understanding.

As a helping professional, you bring your whole self to the process and thereby encourage your clients to do likewise. You can use this book to add a powerful new dimension to your work and create more success and well-being for both you and your clients. By using body-centered coaching you can encourage them to make better choices for themselves. Overall, you can assist clients to pay attention and to honor, trust and make use of the information they receive from their bodies.

> *"Life is only bearable when the mind and the body are in harmony, and there is a natural balance between the two, and each has a natural respect for the other."*
>
> *- D.H. Lawrence*

# 1 ✻ The Power of Listening

Few people have the experience of truly being heard. Fully listening to your clients is a wonderful gift that you can offer them. Listening is a complex activity which involves paying attention at many levels at the same time, so skillful listening takes practice. Being self-aware is the foundation for fully listening to another person.

Your way of *being* as a listener directly impacts your clients and has the power to impact them positively or negatively. Your clients' feelings of safety, trust in self, self-esteem and potential for personal growth can be significantly affected by your level of good will, awareness and expertise as a listener. In this chapter, I will discuss the distinction between empowered and disempowered listening and the impact of each on your clients.

## *Disempowered Listening*

Disempowered listening negatively affects both the client and the coach. When we are listening to our clients, the moment we judge their choices, feel critical of their approach to a problem, compare them from our personal perspective or blame them in any way, we are disempowering them.

We may be caught up in our internal dialog and thinking:

- Oh, boy, here we go again!
- I thought you weren't going to do that.
- I don't think that's possible.
- I wish my life was like yours.

From this way of listening, it is impossible to fully hear the other person because our mind is full of our own reactions. We may be waiting for our turn to speak: being overtly or covertly impatient. We may be wondering if our fee is not enough or too much. We may be caught up in needing to be impressive or clever. This is self-aggrandizing.

As well, the moment we decide that our clients are in need of our help, we are disempowering them. We are no longer focusing on them but on ourselves. We perceive our clients as people who need fixing or need our guidance and advice. All of these thoughts limit our ability to listen and restrict our creativity with them.

*Fixer*

*A fixer has the illusion of being causal.*
*A server knows he/she is being used in the service*
*of something greater, essentially unknown.*

*We fix something specific.*
*We serve always the something:*
*wholeness and the mystery of life.*

*Fixing and helping are the work of the ego.*
*Serving is the work of the soul.*

*When you help, you see life as weak.*
*When you fix you see life as broken.*
*When you serve you see life as whole.*

*Fixing and helping may cure.*
*Service heals.*

*When I help, I feel satisfaction.*
*When I serve, I feel gratitude.*

*Fixing is a form of judgment.*
*Serving is a form of connection.*

*- Author Unknown*

## The Impact of Disempowered Listening

When we are listening in a disempowering way, our clients will have an innate understanding that they are not being heard.

People sense how we feel and what we think about them. They pick it up in their subconscious awareness and they respond accordingly. The information is in the energetic nuances between two people. We may be doing or saying all the right things but internally they will be reacting to the unspoken opinion we have of them. They will know if we are being nice to them for our own purposes rather than caring for them as people. They will intuit that we want to change or manipulate them to see things our way and they will often become resistant to us.

Clients may turn disempowered listening against themselves with thoughts like "I must be really boring for my coach not to want to listen to me." They may start talking louder or faster to be heard. They may stop speaking and become quiet or they may become critical of us, either directly or passively.

> *"The point here is that we can sense how others are feeling toward us. Given a little time, we can always tell when we're being coped with, manipulated, or outsmarted. We can always detect the hypocrisy. We can always feel the blame concealed beneath veneers of niceness. And we typically resent it. It won't matter if the other person tries... sitting on the edge of the chair to practice active listening, inquiring about family members in order to show interest, or using any other skill learned in order to be more effective. What we'll know and respond to is how that person is regarding us when doing those things."*
>
> *- The Arbinger Institute*
> *- Leadership and Self-Deception*

**Exercise:**

Remember a recent time when you were not fully listening to a client. You may have been more concerned with making notes, having judgments or feeling irritable about something that happened in your personal life.

As you remember this incident, ask yourself:

- What was going on in my mind?
- What do I imagine was the impact on my client?
- How fulfilling was this session – for the client and for me?

## *Empowered Listening*

Empowered listening is a way of being, a way of being fully present – body, mind and spirit. Empowered listening is being curious and paying attention to our clients without anything else interfering in the process. With empowered listening we will hear the essence of what is being said and find ourselves whole-heartedly open to our intuition and creativity. We will be more present and receptive and be more natural, appropriate and creative with our responses. It is empowering for both people.

Empowered listening is not passive. Rather, it is being actively intentional, open-hearted, and fully engaged. There is a sense of being totally involved, of participating with our whole being.

> *"When listening to another person, don't just listen with your mind, listen with your whole body. Feel the energy field of your inner body as you listen... You are giving the other person space – space to be. It is the most precious gift you can give."*
>
> *-Eckhart Tolle*
> *- The Power of Now: a Guide to Spiritual Enlightenment*

Empowered listening is profound as well as challenging to learn and practice. It involves a commitment to be the best we can be in service of another human being. As we listen with acceptance we will enjoy our clients, genuinely holding them as creative, resourceful and whole. We know they have their own answers.

Empowered listening of course extends beyond coaching. It's a powerful way to connect at any time.

> *"We have the opportunity many times a day, everyday, to be the one who listens to others, curious rather than certain. But the greatest benefit of all is that listening moves us closer. When we listen with less judgment, we always develop better relationships with each other. It's not differences that divide us. It's our judgments about each other that do. Curiosity and good listening bring us back together."*
>
> *- Margaret Wheatley*
> *- Turning to One Another: Simple Conversations to Restore Hope to the Future*

## *The Impact of Empowered Listening*

The impact of empowered listening on our clients is that they have the rare and cherished experience of being heard; they feel understood and accepted. It is clear that we care about them and this opens space for considerably more depth in their conversations. The person begins to speak from their past experiences, from their present moment experience and from their dreams for the future. They may begin to speak in more depth about things of which they were not previously aware. This unconditional way of listening invites our clients to continue to speak because there is little to resist. As they keep speaking they may become even more powerful in our presence and come to believe and trust that they indeed have their own answers.

Clients will feel safe when they realize that we can be trusted to respect them and see them as whole. Their trust in the connection with us allows for a deepening and strengthening of the coaching alliance. They will begin to connect more and more with their inner strengths and resources. They will connect with the sources of their inspiration, creativity and personal success. This experience can open the door into some insights of their offering to the world: their calling.

### Exercise:

Begin to practice empowered listening. Put aside your other thoughts and listen to your next client with one of these ideas circulating in your mind:

*"This person is very interesting."*

*"This person is unique and creative."*

*"This person is a leader."*

*"This person is saying something of value."*

Notice the impact on the client. Notice the impact on you.

## *Two Possible Scenarios*

### Disempowered Listening

Sam phones and requests an initial session. He briefly describes the problems he is having at home. I listen to him based on my personal filters and opinions and I make up where I think the session will go. We set up an appointment time.

Sam calls at the appointed time. During our dialog, I have an opinion about what needs to happen with his relationship with his wife and am critical about how he's handled the problem so far. I intrude on Sam to ask him questions that lead him to where I think he should be looking. It is impossible for me to hear Sam because my mind is full of my own reactions and opinions about what is being said.

I decide that Sam really needs my help and my expertise. At this point it's all about me and my ability to help: not about Sam. I want to impress him and I think I know THE solution to his dilemma.

Sam has an experience of me as not quite being there for him, not understanding and being judgmental. He has a gut reaction that I want to change or manipulate him. He ends the session and says that he may call me after he thinks about it. He doesn't call.

## Empowered Listening

Sam phones and requests an initial session. He briefly describes the problems he is having at home and I listen from a place of curiosity. I hear him as a human being, a person of value and of worth. I let go of Sam's story line per se and do not make up anything about him. We set up an appointment time and I remain open to our next conversation.

Sam calls at the appointed time. While he is speaking, I am fully listening to him. I provide the space for him to 'land': a place to take refuge, a place to feel heard. I believe Sam has his own answers and I am mindful of listening from a blank slate perspective, noticing what is filling the space.

I listen to Sam from the perspective that he is creative, resourceful and whole: a person with hopes and wishes. I listen from a place of acceptance. He begins to trust. I do not have THE solution for Sam nor do I wish to manipulate him in a certain direction. I am curious and interested in him. I remain unattached and softly focused, paying attention to my intuition. My powerful questions come from this place.

Sam feels heard and understood and is inspired to become clearer about his path. He feels safer and more centered and informs me that he has much more to explore. He books another appointment.

## *Suggestions*

Here are some suggestions as you continue to move towards empowered listening:

- Empowered listening is about wanting to hear: an attitude of the heart. Increase your desire to be a good listener. Make others matter. Be aware of the benefits for both the client and for you.

- Become aware of the areas in your listening that need work. Notice your habits.

- Be gentle and patient with yourself. We all have bad habits when listening. Don't try to be perfect.

- Congratulate yourself on the good listening you are already doing.

- Stay curious: in a place of not knowing. Avoid "knowing the answer". Stay open to possibilities.

- Stay focused on what your client is saying. When you notice your mind wandering, gently bring it back to the present moment.

- Practice silence. Allow your client to finish speaking and be with what they just said. Silence is a discipline. Allow powerful questions to come out of silence and spaciousness. Re-arranged, the letters in 'listen' spell 'silent'.

- Stay connected and mindful to your intuition. Allow powerful questions to come from this place.

- Focus on the client's results, not on yourself as their coach.

- Combine the coaching skill of empowered listening with noticing how you are being with your client. Being in touch with self is the ground for being with another.

- Let go of thinking you need to have the answer. You are

not responsible for your client's answer: they are. This will allow you to be more fully present and relaxed.

- Listen for the resources, for what's right, what's working. Listening for the resources helps clients connect with their resources.
- Practice being aware of listening to what's happening for you, the client and the environment at the same time.

## *Listen*

*When I ask you to listen to me, and you start giving advice, you have not done what I asked.*

*When I ask you to listen to me and you begin to tell me why I shouldn't feel that way, you are trampling on my feelings.*

*When I ask you to listen to me and you feel you have to do something to solve my problem, you have failed me, strange as that may sound.*

*Listen! All I asked was that you listen. Not talk or do – just hear me. Advice is cheap; ten cents will get you both Dear Abby and Billy Graham in the same newspaper. And I can do for myself; I am not helpless. Maybe discouraged and faltering, but not helpless.*

*When you do something for me that I can and need to do for myself, you contribute to my fear and weakness. But, when you accept as a simple fact that I do feel what I feel, no matter how irrational, then I quit trying to convince you and get about the business of understanding what's*

*behind this irrational feeling. And when that's clear,*
*the answers are obvious and I don't need advice.*
*Irrational feelings make sense when we understand*
*what's behind them.*

*Perhaps, that's why prayer works sometimes for*
*people, because God is mute, and "He" doesn't give*
*advice or try to fix things. "He" just listens and lets*
*you work it out for yourself.*

*So, please listen and just hear me. And, if you want*
*to talk, wait a minute for your turn; and I'll listen*
*to you.*

*- Author Unknown*

Empowered listening is nourishing both to your clients and to you. When you are listening to them as being inspired, courageous and creative, then two things happen:

- First, the person has an experience of being received in a meaningful way and experiences the power and worth of really being heard.
- Secondly, you are receiving something that will have a healthy and positive effect on you. By choosing empowered listening you will be increasing your own joy and feelings of gratitude.

Empowered listening is a choice. Finding inspiration in every moment, in every situation, with anyone, will become a powerful and nourishing habit with practice. It means fully noticing the mind-body-spirit experience of being mutually nourished.

# 2 ✺ Contact the Storyteller - Not the Story

When you are listening, there are two potential levels for focus. You can focus on the *story* or you can focus on the *storyteller*.

The story consists of the details about various aspects of your client's life – the who, the where and the what. The story can often be intriguing and interesting and it is very easy to get mesmerized by the details. If you stay focused on the details, however, you may miss the opportunity to connect in an empowered way with your client's inner experience.

Or, you can be curious about the *storyteller* and begin to get a sense of the essence of her or his internal experience. By acknowledging the essence, rather than the details, you provide the opportunity for the client to feel heard and understood in new ways.

## Contact Statements

Establishing and maintaining connection with your clients throughout the session is paramount. Keeping in contact helps you to build relationship and establishes the opportunity for your clients to open up more easily and expansively. There are effective ways of responding that maintain contact.

Non-verbal responses can be saying uh-huh or mmmm. In person they may include smiling, nodding or some other appropriate gesture. Verbal responses can be short phrases that are intended to contact clients without interrupting them or altering the flow of their sharing. In the Hakomi method, these are called *contact statements*.

By making contact statements to connect with the storyteller, rather than the story, you are letting your client know that:

- You are listening and present.
- You're interested in a non-judgmental way.
- You understand.
- You're being with them where they are in their experience.
- You're willing to go to greater depth with them.

## Two Step Process for Making Contact Statements

### First, you begin to notice everything.

*With the clients*: Notice the way they tell the story: tone of voice, speed of talking, their focus at the moment, verbal expressions, level of curiosity, degree of emotion or lack of it. Notice whether they are tentative and indecisive or comfortable and at ease. You can notice gestures and posture when coaching in person.

*In yourself:* Notice any body sensation, contraction or expansion, emotions, intuition, changes in breathing, level of mindfulness and being present.

## Second, you make a short contact statement.

A skillful contact statement is short, uncomplicated, and names the essence of the client's inner experience in the present moment. These are *open-ended phrases,* not *questions,* and are said in a curious and tentative manner. Because contact statements are simple and direct, they do not interrupt the client's experience.

Use as few words as possible. Be aware that it's not about reflecting back the content of the story. Thus, you will be engaging with the storyteller, not the story.

Some examples of words or short phrases you may say are:

**For confusion:**

- Not clear
- Hard to understand
- Very puzzling
- Hard to figure out
- Hard to believe
- Somewhat skeptical

**For frustration:**

- Frustrating isn't it
- Frustrated, huh
- Been difficult for you

**For a good feeling:**

- Feels good
- Nice to hear
- Enjoying yourself

**For any feeling: (naming the feeling)**

- Feeling angry, huh (surprised, excited, anxious, sad)
- Choked up
- Seems like you're a little sad
- That's painful for you
- Frightening, huh
- Pretty upsetting
- That brings up some feeling

**Overwhelming feelings:**

- Lots of feelings there
- Really holding on
- It's hard work
- Hard to let go
- Terrifying

**Around content:**

- I hear you
- Important that you're being heard
- You really wanted that
- Something going on there
- That's powerful for you
- I notice
- Something is changing
- I have a sense of that

- So you're wondering about that
- A real concern for you
- So you're remembering that now

**Emotional stress:**

- Holding your breath
- A lot of feelings
- Tightening up

**As client relaxes:**

- Quieting down
- Going inside
- Feels good to talk about that

Your contact statements are always open to correction. You are willing to be wrong, so if you are off the mark, let it go. You may say to a client, "Feeling sad, huh" and they may respond with, "It's not so much sad, it's more like disappointment." They may deny or refine what you say. The client is always right.

## Using Intuition to Make Contact with What Is Not Being Said

Suzan Bond, author of *Boost Your Intuitive Intelligence*, defines intuition as "direct and immediate knowledge. It's information that you receive without the benefit of analytical reasoning or rational thought." Intuition has a physical resonance or internal harmony to it. The knowing is quiet: having no charge to it.

As mentioned in the introduction, intuition is often called "sixth sense", "inner knowing", "gut reaction" or "still small voice". It can be a shift in energy, a visual image, an emotion or bodily sense.

When I intuit a 'rightness' either in what my client is saying or doing, I get goose-bumps all over my body.

Sometimes your contact statements will come purely from your intuition. These may refer to something the client is already aware of or it may come as a surprise to them. You may have a sense of knowing – that there's something unnamed between the lines, or missing from, or hidden beneath – and decide to contact that. Making contact from intuition involves trusting yourself and taking a risk. You may fear naming your intuition and stay silent, thereby doing your client a disservice.

> *"Many people find their intuition in the body... You may 'see' your intuition in a visual way or feel it kinesthetically.... Whatever your access point, eventually you'll need to verbalize the nudge from your intuition. You make sense out of the sensation by giving words to it. Let's be absolutely clear about this: Your responsibility as a coach is to speak what your intuition gives you. Having intuition and not using it in the coaching relationship is giving only part of the service the client wants from coaching."*
>
> *- Whitworth, Laura et al*
> *– Co-Active Coaching: New Skills for Coaching People Toward Success in Work and Life*

Remember, your intuition is never wrong; your interpretation of it might be, however. Stay with the principle of being curious, tentative and not absolutely certain about it.

## *Client Story*

> *Here is an example of a contact statement based on intuition.*

Jessica had just returned from visiting Elaine, her sister. Elaine had just had a baby a month ago and Jessica was talking about how much fun they had being with each other and with the baby. She was talking in an up-beat way. As I paid attention to my own body sensations, I noticed a feeling in my solar plexus and I had a hunch about what it may be indicating. I tentatively made this short contact statement, "Brought up a longing." I noticed Jessica's intake of breath and I stayed quiet for a few moments to give her space to be with it. Jessica said, "Wow, that went right to my heart."

When you make a contact statement in this way, a client can say, "Yes that's true." Or they can say, "No, that doesn't fit." Either way, the client is right. Your client also chooses whether or not to be coached around the issue at this time.

Making good contact statements is a life skill. They can enhance your coaching and they may also enhance your personal relationships. By responding to essence, rather than content, you let people know that they are being heard.

# 3 ✺ Begin Within

It is important for you to have some personal experience and knowledge of the *begin within* process. The more you are self-aware and in touch with your body experience, the more easily you can encourage your clients to have an awareness of their mind-body-spirit inter-connections. You become more connected with your true center when you shift away from ordinary awareness to self-awareness or what I call *'being-awareness'*. It involves being in the present moment and accessing your intuition. We all have a natural ability to notice and that ability gets better with practice.

> *"We may be barely in touch with our body, unaware of how it is feeling most of the time. As a consequence we can be insensitive to how our body is being affected by the environment, by our actions, and even by our own thoughts and emotions.... When we are more in touch with our body as a result of paying attention to it systematically, we will be far more attuned to what it is telling us and better equipped*

*to respond appropriately. Learning to listen*
*to your own body is vital to improving your*
*health and the quality of your life."*

- *Jon Kabat-Zinn*
- *Full Catastrophe Living: Using the Wisdom of Your Body*
*and Mind to Face Stress, Pain and Illness*

To **begin within** is to be open to an experience and a way of knowing that is beyond the conscious mind. It is an opening to new information and new perspectives; it's the study of a wider range of experience and sensation.

## Mindfulness: An Experience Within

The first step to cultivating greater self-awareness is through an experience, a *state of being* called mindfulness. This is different from our ordinary consciousness. In mindfulness, you are participating as an *observer* of your own behavior and cultivating that part of the mind that can *impartially witness* whatever you are experiencing – body sensations, emotions, impulses, thoughts or memories – without trying to control or direct what is being noticed. It is a way of noticing that is calmly aware of the moment-to-moment flow of present experiences without being identified with them. Mindfulness is used to deepen and stabilize your bodily experiences for greater clarity and insight and to gain a greater sense of well-being.

Mindfulness is an open, non-judgmental way of being with whatever is happening around you and within you. As it involves a non-attachment to particular outcomes, it is sometimes called "choiceless awareness." It involves stepping back from the habitual patterns of judging and reacting: accepting whatever is there without trying to make something happen. It's about letting go and letting be.

> "*Mindfulness is 'willfully passive'. We deliberately decide to observe present experience without interfering with it. This receptive attitude, if exercised for only a few moments at a time, can yield rich insights. Finally, attention during mindfulness is, for the most part, turned inward.*"
>
> Ron Kurtz
> - Body-Centered Psychotherapy:
> the Hakomi Method

## The Practice of Mindfulness

In order to nurture the experience of mindfulness, here are eight practices. Sit comfortably with your feet on the floor and close your eyes. The mere action of closing your eyes and becoming mindful changes your body's physiology and often has a calming effect. This makes it easier to notice sounds and physical sensations and it's also easier to notice your thoughts. It is a way to begin to turn inward and to clear a space for your observer, your internal witness, to notice your present moment experience.

1.  **Breathing Awareness**: Just notice the movement of breath into and out of your body, without needing to breathe in any particular way. Notice the movement of the breath, the rhythm of the inhalation and exhalation, the sensation of breath in the nostrils and in the throat. Without trying to change anything, just become aware of your own breathing, of how your breathing is automatic.

2.  **Exhale – Pause Breathing**: After noticing your breathing for awhile, add a little pause after each exhalation. Just wait for a moment before the next breath comes in.

3.  **Counting Breaths**: This is as simple (not easy!) as it sounds. Count your breaths and every time your mind wanders, start again at number one. You could count each inhalation or exhalation, or inhale – one, exhale – two and so on. Again, the idea is to be relaxed and just focus on present experience.

4.  **Shoulder Shrug**: Follow your breathing rhythm for a moment and then begin to slowly shrug your shoulders up to your ears as you inhale, relax them down again on the exhalation. Release your shoulders several times. Then just relax.

5.  **Hand Squeeze**: As you feel your breath coming in, slowly make a tight fist with one or both hands, curling the fingers in tightly. As you exhale, relax your hand, stretching the fingers wide.

6.  **Body Scanning**: Begin by noticing your breathing for a moment to quiet the mind and bring your attention into the present. Then very slowly and gradually move your attention throughout your body from your feet to your head. Notice the places that feel tense and the places that feel comfortable, soft or relaxed. Take time to explore what you notice in each part of the body. When your attention has come up to your head, you can move it slowly back

down through your body again. Notice if the same places feel tense or if there is a difference. You might move your attention this time into more internal parts of your body, as if you could feel which organs have the sensation of being more or less relaxed. This is just an exploration and a discovery. There is nothing you need to do or change. Simply scan your whole body this way for several minutes.

7. **Noticing**: Begin to turn your attention to the sounds around you for a minute or so. Notice the ones that are close by and then listen for sounds that are further away. Gradually become aware of your breathing, just noticing the breath coming in and the breath going out. Notice other body sensations, and at the same time, be aware of the thoughts and images and ideas that occur. The moment is not a static point, it flows. One thing after another comes into your present moment awareness. Let them come and let them go, like the breath.

8. **The Gap**: In mindfulness, shift your attention away from the activity and the meaning of your thoughts. Just notice that there is a gap between the thoughts: a space between where one thought ends and the other begins. Notice that there is a silence and there's nothing there. OR, it may be difficult to notice a gap because your thoughts are overlapped and there is no gap. In that case, just become aware of the silent background behind your thoughts – much like seeing a page of typewritten words and just noticing all of the white space behind the words

– or noticing a number of sailboats on the ocean
and then putting your attention to the water
surrounding the sailboats – or being aware of
the gaps between the musical notes.

Being mindful is an empowering life skill. It invites you to stop
and pay attention, even for a moment. Jon Kabat-Zinn calls it "the
art of conscious living" or "heartfulness." As you become mindful,
you allow yourself to be more fully in your body and to pay
attention to your heart. As you listen to and trust your heart's
contribution, you have a greater connection with the spirit within
you.

> *"Wisdom arises from peacefulness and
> produces more peace. The wisdom within you,
> as intuition or insightfulness, becomes more
> available to you when you are quiet, calm and
> centered. Learning to relax the body and quiet
> the mind is essential."*
>
> *- Donna Martin*
> *- Remembering Wholeness: InSight Methods*

## Using Mindfulness with Your Clients

*Body-Centered Coaching* is focused on how you can encourage
your clients to experience self-awareness through the body. By
having them begin within, you are supporting them to increase
their awareness of the inherent wisdom of their bodies and of
their intuition as a means to integrate body, mind and spirit.
Mindfulness is the key to all of the client stories.

Although mindfulness and body awareness can be used in a
variety of situations, there are two basic ways that mindfulness

has been used in the client stories. One way is using mindfulness and the study of body signals *any time* during a session when it is appropriate. The other is to use mindfulness as a prelude to study a specific experience *as an experiment.* Here's an overview.

*Any time:* Clients may be relating a situation and you may ask, "While you're telling me this, what is happening in your body?" As clients pause to check in with their body, you can suggest they close their eyes, go inward and be still in order to help them to notice. In this situation, mindfulness spontaneously happens and gives clients an immediate opportunity to pay attention to their body, often offering them another perspective.

In these moments clients may be calm and quiet or may be in the midst of overwhelming emotions such as agitation, panic, or anger. As the coach, you guide clients to become mindful by being calm yourself. The more agitated or overwhelmed clients are, the more they may need their coach to guide them through the process. Therefore, it's important for you to talk more slowly and be mindful yourself.

*As an Experiment:* Having a client become mindful may be used as a prelude to running an experiment. Inherent in this is an attitude of curiosity and a willingness to 'not know' and to be surprised. You prepare your clients to study their experiences. The following chapter – Experimenting with Possibilities – has a client story and detailed steps for the process of setting up an experiment. Basically, you set the stage for your clients to become mindful, ask them to pay attention to their breathing, allow some time for them to shut out the visuals around them and begin to focus within. Here is a simple script that you can use to assist your clients to become mindful.

**Mindfulness Script:**

> *"Close your eyes and begin to turn your attention to your breathing: not trying to change anything, simply noticing your breath. (pause) Notice how your breath comes in and your breath goes out. (pause) On your next exhalation, allow more of your body weight to sink into your chair, knowing it is there to support you. (pause) Take as much time as you need."*

Adapt the script to meet your specific needs. Be sure to use a calm, neutral and soothing voice, being aware of slowing down your speech. You will be offering your clients a way of noticing with their whole being: ears, eyes, feelings, heart, body and spirit. You are offering them the opportunity to be like a still pond, receptive and quiet and fully listening. For this to happen there needs to be an alliance between client and coach, based on trust and respect. Respect is something that has to be given. By offering respect to your clients, you are giving them a gift. Respect is in the giving, not in the receiving.

## Feeling vs. Sensing

Throughout the client examples in this book, the word *feeling* is used very selectively. Because the word *feeling* is used in a number of different ways, to describe various ways of experiencing, the word *feeling* can be confusing when asking questions related to the body.

"I feel tired." or "I feel nauseous." – describe body experiences.

"I feel like going to a movie." – describes a desire or a want.

"I feel like screaming." – describes an impulse.

"I feel sad." – describes an emotion, often accompanied by a story.

"I feel lonely." – implies a whole story about what or who is missing.

When feeling is experienced with the body alone, it can be called more accurately a sensation or "sensing". This is an important distinction for coaches who are accessing the body. Asking a question like, "What are you sensing in your body?" or "What is the energy you notice in your body?" eliminates confusion for the client as to what you are asking. If you were to ask, "What are you feeling in your body?" the client may interpret that to mean what emotion is there. Emotions have different qualities to them so we distinguish them by naming them or by using a metaphor. Sensations are the language of the body.

# 4  Experimenting with Possibilities

There are a number of ways to gather information from the body. The technique of *Experimenting with Possibilities* can be used in a variety of situations. This is described in detail following the client story. *Experimenting with Possibilities* is used with the intention to gather information, which may or may not result in a definitive decision.

## Client Story

> *In this client story, Jodie wants to expand on her insights to fine tune the possibilities for the direction of her coaching practice. She wants to access her body's wisdom. She knows in her heart that she won't feel fulfilled if she ignores what she truly wants.*

Jodie is an eclectic, multi-talented, life-time learner who has recently completed her coaching certification. Her background has included teaching at the high school level, being a body worker in a therapeutic massage clinic and working in a large corporation as an administrative assistant. She has a wide range of interests.

Jodie has determined that it is important to focus on a specialized niche for her coaching practice. She came to the call overwhelmed by the number of possibilities and was in search of more clarity and direction.

In conversation, we came up with some possibilities with which to experiment. We decided to ask her body for whatever information it had to contribute to the variety of choices at hand. The goal was to narrow down the possibilities, not necessarily to make a committed decision.

Her broad list of choices included:

- coaching *educators* who want to make a difference in the school system by addressing burn-out issues.
- coaching *body-workers* as she has training as a massage therapist.
- coaching life balance using her training in the *Myers-Briggs* assessment tool.
- coaching parents of children with *ADD* (Attention Deficit Disorder) because her daughter has ADD.

I explained the process – mindfulness, noticing, signaling, reporting and shaking it off – which you'll find outlined following the story. The *key* is to take time in between each possibility. This allows the client the space to let go of any preceding attitudes or insights. It clears the energy and makes room for new learning.

Coach:  (in a calm, neutral voice) Close your eyes and begin to turn your attention to your breathing… (pause) not trying to change anything… simply noticing your breath… (pause) Notice how your breath comes in and your breath goes out… (pause) On your next exhalation, allow more of your body weight to sink into your chair… knowing it is there to support you… (pause) Take as much time as you need… When you are ready, give me the signal we agreed upon and I will begin.

Jodie:  (pause) Uh, huh.

Coach:  **Notice what happens when I say… (pause)… Myers-Briggs.**

Jodie:  (pause) I noticed a ho-hum feeling. I like the instrument a lot… and I feel bored with it.

Coach:  Did you notice anything else in your body?

Jodie:  Yes, my shoulders drooped and I have a sense of being deflated, like air going out of a balloon. There's not much energy here.

Coach:  Good noticing. Anything else?

Jodie:  No, that's it for now.

Coach:  Take some time to shake off what we just talked about. (pause) Go back to noticing your breathing, becoming mindful again. (pause) Take as much time as you need and let me know when ready for another possibility.

Jodie:   (pause) Uh, huh.

Coach:   **Notice what happens when I say**... (pause)...
**educators**.

Jodie:   My heart rate quickened. I feel excited and I have a 'go
for it' in my body.

Coach:   Good noticing. Anything else you want to report?

Jodie:   No, it's a good feeling though.

Coach:   Take some time to shake off what we just talked about.
(pause) Go back to noticing your breathing, becoming
mindful again. (pause) Take as much time as you
need and let me know when you're ready for another
possibility.

Jodie:   (pause) Uh, huh.

Coach:   **Notice what happens when I say**... (pause)... **ADD.**

Jodie:   No way. Absolutely not!

Coach:   That sounds pretty clear.

Jodie:   Yeah, I'm surprised at my response.

Coach:   What did you notice in your body?

Jodie:     I stomped my foot on the floor.

Coach:    Good noticing. Take some time to shake off what we
          just talked about. (pause) Go back to noticing your
          breathing, becoming mindful again. (pause) Take as
          much time as you need and let me know when you're
          ready for another possibility.

Jodie:     (pause) Uh, huh.

Coach:    **Notice what happens when I say** (pause)…**body-
          workers.**

Jodie:     Hmm. I feel a heart connection to that group of like-
          minded people. I can feel the warmth in my body and
          my caring for them. I'm not sure what exactly the focus
          would be but it definitely feels like it has potential.

Coach:    Great noticing. Anything else?

Jodie:     No, that feels complete for now.

Coach:    Take some time to shake off what we just talked about.


This experiment in mindfulness helped Jodie to let go of two of
the categories. It gave her a more condensed list from which to
work. Experiments in mindfulness could have further application
as her process of discovery continues in later sessions. Although it
appears short to read, the process of identifying the 'possibilities',
delivering them and coaching in relation to them took a full
session of forty minutes.

## The General Steps: Experimenting with Possibilities

1. In conversation, you discover that there are some possibilities to explore surrounding an issue and decide to check in with your client's body to see what other information exists.

2. Together, you make a list of the possibilities and you record them on paper. You agree on a shortened key phrase that captures the essence of the possibility. As an example, the client was considering working with educators who want to make a difference in the school system. The possibility was shortened down to the single word 'educators'. Also, let your client know that when you say the possibilities later they will not be in the same order as recorded.

3. You let the client know what to expect by describing the following steps to them:

   - *Mindfulness* – See previous chapter for a full description, including the experimental attitude. Both coach and client need to be mindful in the process.

   - *Noticing* – Let clients know that when being mindful they **may notice a thought, a feeling, a sensation, an image, a memory, or tension in the body.** It may be anything at all or there may be nothing to notice. This is intended as self-study with no 'right answer'.

- *Signaling* – Arrange a signal with your clients that will let you know that they are ready. On the phone it may be something like 'uh-huh' or 'ready'. In person it may be something like raising a hand.

- *Reporting* – Let clients know that they can report anything they notice and you will write it down for later conversation. Let them know that this is a stage of reporting only. It's not meant to be interpretive, although some conversation about what's being observed may occur.

- *Shaking it off* – Let clients know that in between possibilities, you will have them shake off the previous possibility. Let them know it's their opportunity to clear the energy that is created and to let go and remain un-attached. For some 'shaking it off' is merely the intention of clearing their energy. For others, it can mean doing something physical such as flicking their hands. It's an individual choice.

4. You invite clients to be mindful and when they give you the signal that they are ready, you begin to 'deliver' the possibilities, one at a time.

   - *Coach's notes:* Deliver the possibilities in a tone of voice that is careful and neutral and have your voice subside at the end. Your timing should be measured: slow,

evenly spaced and intentional. Begin
every sentence with the same words:

*"Notice what happens when I say
(pause)............"*

5.  Clients may respond immediately or they may
    be silent for a few moments. Give them time. If
    they don't initiate a response, then ask, "What
    did you notice?" Every answer is right and
    recorded; it's the clients' felt experience.

    This part may take clients away from being
    mindful and conversation may occur. This is
    **not**, however, the place for coaching about any
    of the responses. That will happen later.

6.  Have clients shake off each one, whatever that
    feels like for them. Coach them back into being
    mindful and have them give you the signal
    that they are being mindful and are ready for
    another possibility.

When the experiments are complete, you can coach your clients to
find their own  meanings and interpretations of the results. The
clients have their own answers. Stay curious and use empowered
listening.

The number of opportunities for using this technique is limitless. Use your imagination to create experiments with your clients. They may want to:

- Prioritize their values. You could invite mindfulness to experiment with the impact of each value. They could notice the ones that have the greatest impact.
- See what rings true with their passion or purpose statements.
- Choose the wording for their business cards, brochures or other marketing materials.
- Become clear on their offering or where to advertise.
- Experiment with different possibilities for transition or career change.
- Make decisions: notice the impact of each option.
- Become clear on prioritizing – identify the first steps in a process.
- Check in with the body's language and wisdom on any topic.

This body-centered technique helps clients discover information that is not readily available through the intellect. Clients may report a myriad of things they have noticed.

Here are a few examples:

- *Body:* throat tightness, heart opening, tightness in chest, smile on face, knot in stomach, sour taste in mouth, sticky fingers, an itch, warmth, tingle in arms.

- *Breath:* took my breath away, became shallow, became constricted, became fuller, opened up, became deeper. Any change can be significant.

- *Images:* expressed literally or as metaphors.

- *Emotion:* fear, sadness, obligation, good feeling, relief, want to cry, ho-hum, excitement, any emotion.

- *Hear:* screeching gulls, an intuitive message, a voice like a father saying, "You can do it."

- *Nothing:* neutral, no noticeable response.

- *Sense of:* holding back, softening, making an effort to feel positive, moving forward, the sky's the limit.

The interpretation is up to the client. Be curious about the meaning they find for whatever they notice, and how it can be integrated. It's all great material for coaching.

# 5 ✻ Decision-Making

Clients often come to the coaching call needing to make a decision. Generally, there are many influences during the decision-making process:

- The intellect is often dominant; we make 'pro' and 'con' lists, make rationalizations, and label things good or bad, right or wrong.
- There is often the added pressure to make decisions based on what we think we *should* do, rather than on what we *want* to do.
- We may be operating from what used to be true for us but is no longer the case.
- We may be making decisions based solely on what we think and discounting or ignoring our intuition.

From these perspectives, decision-making is *reactive* rather than *responsive* to the realities of the moment. Being *reactive* is our habitual, knee-jerk reflex reaction to an event. Being *responsive* happens as we pause to stand back from our initial reaction and make choices that are in alignment with our total being – body, mind and spirit. It's a way to be discerning when making choices. Discernment is based on being mindful and intentional in order to have a deeper understanding. There is often calmness and no 'charge' involved. When we're coming from our inner knowing we can operate from greater truth. And that may be independent of our analytical mind or our current belief system.

> *"The critical challenge of discernment... requires that we also tread a path between two essential questions: 'What is right for me?' and 'Where am I willing to be led?' The most critical discernment skill is being able to distinguish between the sound of integrity and the sound of its absence. In order to recognize a true call, you must be able to recognize a false one, just as in order to spot a truth you must be able to spot a lie... the discernment process is about being actively patient, using the time we have to submit the evidence we gather to the compassionate scrutiny of the mind, the adjudication of the heart, the gut reaction of the body."*
>
> *- Gregg Levoy*
> *- Callings: Finding and Following*
> *an Authentic Life*

A perspective is a way of looking at something; this is different from an option. An option is something *to do*, while a perspective is a *way to be, a way to think about something, a way to 'see' something or a feeling*. It is important, therefore, for your client to experience the *beingness* of a perspective by embodying it. Your client can 'try on' a perspective, which often accesses their intuition. The body has a different way of giving you needed information from its own perspective.

# Client Story

*In the following story, you will witness how Ted connected with his inner knowing in order to arrive at a clear decision for himself.*

Ted came to the call and indicated that he was 'stressed out'. He was faced with a decision about whether or not to accept a position overseas for a year. It was a splendid opportunity for advancement in his career but he was torn about leaving his family for such a long period of time.

We decided to take time to be with each of the various perspectives in relation to his decision. Ted began with one perspective and as we were finished with one, we would identify another one to embody. Each time we completed a perspective, I had Ted move his body to a new location in the room. This was analogous to 'shaking off a possibility' in the previous chapter. We kept doing this process until Ted had exhausted his list. As he tried on each perspective he was able to step into the experience of that particular view and notice signals from his body.

The first perspective was: *"I'm interested in different cultures."*

As Ted embodied this one, he noticed a contraction in his body. He realized the impact of living in a culture that was overcrowded: where respect for personal space is not always acknowledged. His body felt claustrophobic. We studied the sensations of that and stayed curious about everything that showed up.

The second perspective was: *"I'm not a city person."*

Ted talked about his love of nature and his current lifestyle which included many outdoor activities. He experienced fear in his abdomen as he felt the anxiety of possibly watching too much TV and not being able to find green space easily. His shoulders drooped and he had a collapsed posture.

The third perspective was: *"I am alone."*

Ted's body caved in as he experienced the sensation of being all alone in a foreign country away from his family and friends. He felt very uncomfortable in his body. He had the sensation of 'fight or flight'.

The fourth perspective was: *"I'll make lots of money."*

As Ted checked in with his body, he noticed it felt neutral. Nothing much was going on. He mentioned that he had expected more of an uplifting feeling but it just wasn't there.

The fifth perspective was: *"Re-entry will be tough."*

As he felt into the experience of returning home and re-connecting with his wife and children, he noticed a lot of tension in his shoulders. It felt disquieting to him.

The sixth perspective was: *"My family is really important to me."*

Ted began speaking about his teenage son; he felt warmth running through his body and a sense of relief. He connected with his longing to be with his son throughout his teenage years and share experiences.

The seventh perspective was: *"I love being in community."*

Ted spoke of his current community – people in his neighborhood, in his church and at his sports club. He felt an expansion in his arms and they spontaneously went out to the side as if offering a large welcome. His body felt calm and relaxed. He felt fully alive.

The eighth perspective was: *"I have a lot of allergies."*

Ted spoke about health, pollution, and medical considerations. He felt a knot in his stomach.

As Ted stood back from his experience of the perspectives, he said that the process had the feeling of trying on different cloaks. Ted realized that he didn't want to go overseas for a year, no matter what. His parting words were, *"Thank you. I am very clear on my decision now. If I hadn't experienced my body's response to the perspectives, I would have always wondered if I had made the right decision. Now I can totally let that go and happily and fully commit to staying here."*

## *Waiting for Clarity*

Often there is some elevated emotion about making a decision.

- We think that if we make the decision 'right now' the anxiety will go away. That is often not the case. When we make a decision simply because we're anxious, we do not honor ourselves by allowing time for clarity.
- Or, we think that we have to make the decision immediately just because someone has posed a question. We don't allow ourselves time to think. This scenario can

often happen on the telephone when someone calls to invite us somewhere. Rather than saying, "I need time to think about this... I'll call you back," we often say "yes" to the request and then wish we hadn't committed ourselves.

- Or, a decision gets made when we are excited about possibilities. We forget to take the time to pay attention to our body's wisdom. When we hurry, we can make decisions without paying full attention to what we really want. Instead, we decide about what seems like a good idea in the moment. Later we realize we have made a mistake.

- Or, we make a decision based on desperation. We think thoughts like, "I better grab this opportunity while it's here." This is a knee-jerk reaction and doesn't allow time for concrete information to be gathered. Later we regret the decision.

During a coaching session, there may be an inclination to hurry clients to become clear and make a decision. It comes from wanting to hold our clients accountable and away from procrastination. Problems can be created when clients make decisions under these circumstances. If we collude with our clients under this kind of pressure, the result may not be in their best interest.

There needs to be space within the coaching relationship to have your clients choose to wait – especially when they are unclear and have not reached an inner knowing that feels right for them. You can lead your clients to be mindful and connect with their inner calm and greater peacefulness. Help them access their true values: the inter-connection of body, mind and spirit. In the practice of body-centered coaching, you hold an abundance of information in your awareness. When a client is in the throes of making a decision, remember to hold, as one vital perspective – *When in doubt, WAIT!*

# 6 ✳ Remembering the Resource

*Remembering the resource* is another powerful technique to bring clients into their bodies and be empowered. It helps clients to realign with what has gone right – their resources and their accomplishments. They connect with their internal 'natural resources' – body, mind and spirit – and remember their resilience and strength. *Remembering the resource* creates an empowered feeling which is often accompanied with an image or symbol. It reminds clients about the part of them that can handle many varied situations.

According to Jim Field, Ph.D.,

> *"The empowering question, 'How did you do this?'...encourages the person to take ownership of their own strengths and coping abilities. Similar questioning will help to elicit the pride, of which people are often not aware, in their ability to be resilient and survive, often in very remarkable and positive ways. These strengths and resiliencies acknowledged and*

*affirmed are conducive to building a foundation in the service of engendering, enhancing, and supporting shift experiences. The knowledge that people can make the shift on their own enhances and challenges therapists [coaches] to respect clients and their capacities to do so."*

*- Unpublished doctoral dissertation: "The Experience of the Shift to Internal Authority"*

## Client Story

*In the following story, Leah fully embodied a remembered experience – calling upon her resilience, strength and inner resourcefulness – so she could integrate the learning and move forward.*

There was a difficult situation that was looming for Leah. After some empowered listening and preliminary coaching…

Coach:  I know that you've had many life experiences and have faced difficult situations in the past. I am wondering if you can remember a time when you had to draw on everything you had inside yourself to get through a difficult situation: a time you feel proud about how you handled the situation.

Leah:  Yes, I remember a vivid afternoon in my life. I had gone to the beach feeling 'at my wits end' about my husband's small business. He had worked for many years trying to make a go of it and we were teetering on the edge of financial disaster. I felt both helpless and powerless to support him. I was staring out at the water feeling very depressed and confused.

Coach: I want you to embody the position that you were sitting in at the beach. Go right back to that day, remembering it as if it's happening right now.

Leah: Okay, I'm there. I'm leaning against a rock.

Coach: Leah, allow yourself to fully embody the despair you were feeling that day, as if it is actually happening in this present moment.

Leah: I remember it well. I'm hunched over with my chin in my hands and I just don't have any energy. I feel like crying.

Coach: Sad, huh. (pause) What happens next?

Leah: I am mesmerized by the water and I stare at it for a long time. Then I notice a mother otter swimming close to shore, with three babies swimming beside, over and under her all at once. I jump to my feet to get a better look.

Coach: Jump to your feet right now and tell me what you notice about the otters.

Leah: I am very curious about the mother otter, how she is managing so many activities. She appears to be on guard for predators, at the same time having a plan of where she is going, and patient with all the frolicking of her babies. She is handling it all at once.

Coach: And how does all this noticing impact you?

Leah: In that moment I remember feeling a shift. Then I understood there was a message for me.

Coach: And, what was the message?

Leah: The message was: to play with my children, stop my persistent worrying and let go of material things. All I needed to do was to take charge of the things within my control and let go of the rest.

Coach: Sounds powerful. What's happening in your body right now?

Leah: I'm standing very firmly on my feet, very grounded. My shoulders are back and I'm looking straight ahead. I remember this feeling being the same that afternoon.

Coach: Then what happened?

Leah: I went home knowing that the best way to support my husband while he was dealing with the business was to keep the family environment as stable as possible and take charge of responsibilities over which I had some control. We got through the challenging time together and grew closer in the process.

Coach: Wonderful. Leah, how can you apply this learning and insight to the situation that you came to the call with today?

Leah: Good question. (pause) I guess it's the same learning as back then. I'm reminded to take responsibility for situations within my control – and let go of the things outside of my control. Wow! It feels really good to remember that.

Coach:  Yes, and from this place let's do some coaching around a plan that will fit for you. (And the coaching session continued, building on Leah's connection to her strength.)

To tap into resources, there are many questions that clients can address, either in the coaching session or as an inquiry for them to ponder between sessions. All of these contribute to the empowerment of your client.

Examples are:

- How did I do it? What did I draw on in myself?
- What did I learn about myself in overcoming this challenge?
- What are the strengths and resources I can count on inside myself?
- What skills or techniques did I use to manage my emotions?
- What kept me on track?
- What is the opportunity now?

All clients have resources inside themselves. Bringing those resources into their awareness and embodying them is a profound way to empower your clients.

# 7 ❋ Embodying Key Words

Along with empowered listening, it is important that you listen to the language your clients use. They may use language in the form of metaphors, word pictures and other words or phrases which are expressive. They may say:

- I feel like a giant oak tree with my branches reaching for the sky.
- It was like diving into a pool of freezing water.
- It was like an ogre appearing out of the forest.
- My head feels like a beehive with a swarm of bees buzzing around.

Often the language clients use is representative of how their bodies are feeling and may contain valuable information about how they experience the world.

Language is also indicative of learning style: auditory, visual or kinesthetic. Let's take a "day at the beach" as an example. An *auditory* person learns by hearing so they will tell you how it sounded to them. Their day at the beach could be described by the screeching of the gulls or the sound of the crashing waves. A *visual* learner is picture-based. Their day at the beach could be described by the color of the water or the shapes of the rocks. A *kinesthetic* person learns by touch, feeling and doing. Their day at the beach could be described by the warmth of the sun on their skin or the texture of the sand between their toes. To deepen the experience for your clients, you can begin to ask questions based on their primary modality of learning.

## Client Story

*In body-centered coaching, it is wonderful when you can actually make the experience come alive by taking the words that clients use and having them act them out; either physically or by imagery. Here's an example of Terrie's experience.*

Terrie called and was feeling low. She was experiencing a familiar discontent and said that her old anxiety was returning. She said that she felt helplessly trapped with no options and that she had *'painted herself into a corner'*.

After a few minutes of empowered listening, I suggested that she stand up and literally move to stand facing a corner in her office. As we were on the phone, I had her describe the things that she was noticing about the corner: anything from the sensation, the feel, the texture, the look, the color. Terrie mindfully reported what she was noticing.

When I asked her what she was sensing in her body, she spoke of being squished in a corner and an awareness of tension. I had her exaggerate the situation by literally having her jam her body into the corner, feeling the walls against her shoulders. This exacerbated her sense of being trapped and increased the perception of being pressured to stay there.

I acknowledged her 'being trapped' and encouraged her to keep tuning into her body. As she stood there she had the sense that she was not allowing herself to enjoy her strengths and was putting too much of a burden on herself. She hung her head and was leaning against the walls of the corner.

Terrie also had a physical sense that there was an actual dark line that had been drawn behind her, not allowing her to back up. She felt even more trapped now. When asked about the purpose of the line, she had an image of her mother telling her to behave and do things in a certain way… or else! As she kept noticing, she spoke about the impact of what she called 'limiting rules of conduct'. She had a heightened awareness of her anxiety about doing things that women aren't 'supposed' to do. She spoke about her fear of people's judgments concerning her decisions.

I drew attention to how she had colluded with the 'nay-sayers' and become a participant in holding the line in place. She immediately recognized the implications of that. Then she realized the good news: that she had choices. Asking her what 'having choices' would be like, she embodied standing in that perspective – noticing her body straighten and her head lift – and gradually the dark line became more and more faint.

When Terrie was ready to move 'out of the corner', we designed how she would turn very slowly and mindfully and speak the following words out loud. *"I can create whatever I want. I can do it my own way."* She embodied her powerful language and stepped away from the corner.

She breathed into this new perspective. I acknowledged her courage and her persistence to create the life she loves. She knew that she could once again embrace her life fully.

There are beautiful gems to be mined when working with a client's words. Their chosen words are not only rich in meaning for them but provide a wonderful background from which to embody the inter-connection of body, mind and spirit.

# 8 ✳ The Power of Beliefs

Beliefs can be *empowering*, encouraging limitless possibilities in our lives. OR, beliefs can be *disempowering*, encouraging us to settle for limited possibilities in our lives. Beliefs form patterns of thoughts or attitudes that we have about ourselves and influence how we interpret our world. They are the filters through which we respond to life – creating our reality, thereby creating our behavior. Beliefs can work *for* us or they can work *against* us.

> *"My beliefs I test on my own body, on my intuitional consciousness, and when I get a response there, then I accept."*
>
> *- D.H. Lawrence*

Beliefs are created by us. The process begins subconsciously early in life. They are a generalized way that we began to see the world and then looked for evidence to prove our belief. Then they became self-fulfilling prophesies, positive or negative. Beliefs can be learned from what others have said to us or from personal experience.

## Empowering Beliefs

When beliefs are working for you, they are empowering and they affirm that so much more is possible. Empowering beliefs have the power to positively shape your reality, influence your behavior and help to create the results that you want in your life. Empowering beliefs influence you emotionally and physiologically. They improve your ability to perform effectively, undertake challenges and stay focused.

Some examples of empowering beliefs are:

- I am competent.
- I trust the decisions I make.
- I deserve to have a great life.
- I am confident and self-assured.
- I celebrate my uniqueness.
- I can make the money I need by doing work that I love.

## Disempowering Beliefs

When beliefs are disempowering and limiting, they work against you. They too have the power to influence your reality, your behavior and the subsequent results – in a negative way however. They influence you emotionally and physiologically. They decrease your ability to perform effectively, undertake challenges and stay focused. They undermine and hold you back. 'Inner critic' or 'gremlin' are other words for disempowering beliefs. They become ingrained and habitual and you subconsciously or consciously believe they are true.

Some examples of limiting beliefs are:

- No matter how hard I try, it's never good enough.
- I can't trust people to support me.
- What I do isn't really important.
- My opinion doesn't matter.
- I'm too much.
- I'm not enough.
- I will never make a living as a coach.

Here are some ways that you can spot disempowering beliefs in your clients:

- in the language they use: "I could never... I don't know how... It only happens to other people... It's always the same... It will never happen... I can't do this."
- by their lack of energy which can show up in their tone of voice or in their description of their energy... their body language (which you can 'hear' on the phone with empowered listening)
- their 'stuckness' in having only one way of seeing something
- in expressions of fear or in their energy of fear
- repetitive behavior that isn't working

## Client Story

*In the following client story, Bonnie embodied her disempowering belief, noticed her behavior and the results she was creating. Ultimately, she embodied an empowering belief that allowed her to respond differently and create a different result when in front of a group.*

Bonnie came to the call overwhelmed. She is a teacher who had been asked by her principal to present a seminar series about how to teach the new science program. The series was to be presented, at a district level, to her colleagues. She was on a team with three other high-powered teachers. During the first seminar, Bonnie felt chained to her power point presentation. It provided a false sense of security for her. She noticed that she was not contributing as much as she could for fear of making a mistake or looking foolish, especially in front of her peers.

I had Bonnie stand up and close her eyes, see herself in front of the group and allow the full feeling of *overwhelm* to surface. Bonnie felt like a fraud in front of the team. I had her embody the behavior and the internal language of 'being a fraud'. She reported that her shoulders were hunched. She had many judgments and criticisms of herself. She repeatedly thought *"Who do I think I am?"* The results she created when caught in this *disempowering belief* were predictable. She was not connected with the participants and she was not allowing herself to be inspiring to them or to her team. She felt the full impact of all those dynamics.

I asked her, "What results do you want?" She talked about being a leader who is relaxed about being herself and being as approachable as a good friend. I had her experiment with embodying this. She took her time. She reported that her knees felt looser and she instinctively started playfully swaying back and forth. Her shoulders were relaxed, and she imagined that she was wearing playful clothes with lots of bright colors. When I had her embody 'playful and fun', she immediately felt more like herself.

I asked, "From here, what do you believe about being in front of the group?" She said *"This is fun. I can be myself."* This became her *empowering belief*. As a way of reminding herself to be playful, and as a way of feeling more authentically like herself, she decided to leave her long, black skirt and neutral colors at home and to wear more colourful clothes and playful jewellery to the next presentation.

A week later, Bonnie reported that the presentation had indeed been fun. When the old belief tried to sneak in, she merely noticed what she was wearing and remembered to be playful and her easy-going self. She received a lot of positive feedback from the team and the participants. Several people commented on her aliveness and spontaneity. They appreciated that she could make the learning fun. Bonnie's modelling reminded the participant teachers that by being themselves in the classroom it would make learning more fun for their students.

When working with disempowering beliefs, it is important to have your clients fully embody the limiting belief; invite them into the body language, reiterate the self-talk, and have them experience the negative results – the whole thing. Then, by focusing on the results they want to create, have them embody that perspective, once again using the body language and alternate self-talk to create a new empowering belief.

> *"You will always be afraid of hearing the question 'Who do you think you are?' until you are able to answer that question for yourself. When you decide to make your personal and spiritual development a top priority by creating a rock solid relationship with yourself, you*

*gain the power and confidence to make your greatest contribution to the world. You stop caring so much about what others think and start caring more about who you are becoming and how you will make a difference in the lives of others. You shift from being self-involved to confident, courageous, and emotionally strong; the exact qualities you'll need to lead a purposeful life that means something."*

*- Cheryl Richardson*
*- Life Makeover For The Year newsletter*

The practice of body-centered coaching offers the possibility for disempowering beliefs and old patterns of behavior that have been outside of awareness to become conscious. When conscious, they can be changed.

# 9 ✺ Overcoming Con-fusions

Another way of working with the body to access information is through movement and gesture. This technique involves looking at different perspectives and ways that we have concepts *fused* together – creating 'con-*fusion*'. This is based on the idea that bringing something subconscious fully into awareness is a prerequisite for change.

*Con-fusion* refers to the way we have fused two things together in our minds. Much like beliefs, we associate them either by being told they go together or by connections we have made based on our past experiences. An example would be the idea that if we cry it means that we are weak. So, when we shed some tears, we automatically assume that it's a display of weakness.

You can tease out some of your own *con-fusions* by rapidly finishing the following sentences. **Do the exercise quickly at first, without editing.** You want to discover the strong associations you have with certain key words and ideas.

Being *good* means I _____

If I'm *bad* it means that _____

If I feel *powerful* it means _____

If I get *angry,* then _____

When I'm being *responsible,* I _____

To be *free* means that _____

If I'm *fearful* it means that _____

If I get *too successful* then _____

I am a *failure* when _____

As an example, let's associate anger with being hurtful. Your sentence may sound like, "If I get angry, someone will be hurt." The *con-fusion* is that these two things **always** go together. With that fusion in place, it could be difficult for you to express anger or to even admit it. It creates a whole set of expectations and reactions.

When you are working with your clients, listen very carefully for any signs of *con-fusion.* You will hear someone's assumptions and associations more easily when you are aware of how you are with your own *con-fusions.*

Here are some examples of the myriad of *con-fusions* that may exist:

- If I cry it means that I am weak.
- Being powerful means I'm a bully.
- Being a success means that I take advantage of people.
- If I claim my freedom it means that others will suffer.
- If I fail it means I've done something wrong.
- If I get angry, I will hurt somebody.
- When I feel afraid, I'm a sissy.
- To be free means that I will end up alone.
- If I'm successful, people won't like me any more.
- Being good means I have to obey.
- If I'm bad it means I'm neglectful.

Prior to beginning this process with a client, either on the phone or in person, go through a movement exercise as a way of preparing them. Have them practice these actions:

- Clasp their hands together.
- Unclasp their hands and open their arms out to each side.

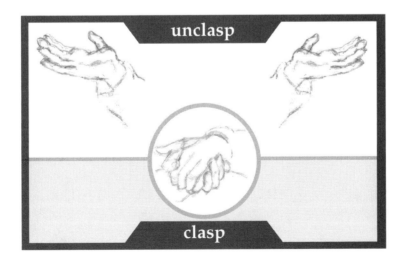

Encourage them to practice each of these movements a few times. When in person, have the client mimic your movements. These actions are significant to the felt sense of the experience. Let them know they will be assigning a word or a concept to each hand.

## Client Story

*Here is a story of how Hettie learned from her con-fusion. As the coach, I recorded Hettie's verbal responses and encouraged her to report on what she was sensing in her body. Make sure to keep the whole exercise slow and deliberate.*

Hettie was having trouble making decisions in relation to her small business. When I asked her what memories she had of decision-making as a child, she spoke of a time when she was eight years old. As the eldest child and responsible for her younger sister, she made a 'bad' decision and was punished for it. She had felt humiliated by her father and unsure of herself.

Hettie didn't like making decisions because if she made a mistake, she would feel humiliated and her self-esteem would suffer. So, whenever possible, she avoided making any decision. Her *con-fusion* was that if she made a wrong decision she would feel worthless. Through our discussion we explored the two concepts she had fused together and shortened them down to *decision-making* and *self-worth*. Here's how we worked with it.

## Part One

Each hand represents a concept. Putting hands together allows the client to have the felt experience of *'equal to'* or *'the same as'*.

Coach:     *When you take **decision-making** (right hand open)
           and **self-worth** (left hand open)*

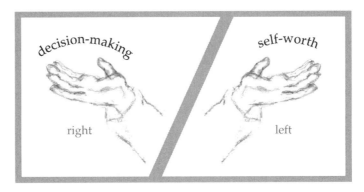

           *and you put them together (clasp hands together),
           what are you CREATING?*

Hettie:    "A state of paralysis. I'm blocked." She reported having
           a knot in her stomach.

Coach: *When you take **decision-making** (right hand open)*
*And **self-worth** (left hand open)*

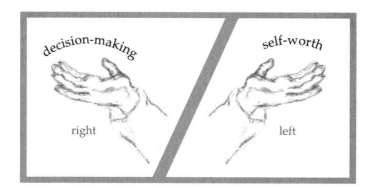

*and you put them together (clasp hands together),*
*what are you NOT CREATING?*

Hettie: "The opportunity for creative expression and room
for the bubbly person I can often be." She spoke of
everything feeling heavy in her body.

Coach:  *When you take **decision-making** (right hand open)*
*and **self-worth** (left hand open)*

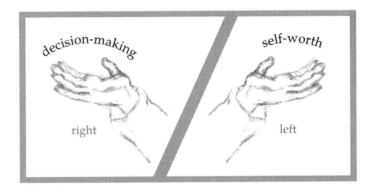

*and you put them together* (clasp hands together),
*what are you RESISTING?*

Hettie:  "Me. Possibilities. Open doors. The part that wants to
be brave, to do things others haven't done. Be a trail
blazer." She felt a sense of sadness when she realized
she had made up the rule: "Decisions have to be right...
or else!"

**Part Two**

Each hand represents a concept. Separating the hands allows the client to have the felt experience of '**NOT** *equal to*' or '**NOT** *the same as*'.

Coach:   *When you take **decision-making** and **self-worth***
         (hands clasped together)

         *and you separate them.*
         (unclasp hands and open arms to each side),
         *what are you CREATING?*

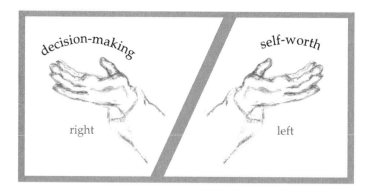

Hettie:   "Space. Possibilities. An open attitude. More fun. Less pressure." The sensation she reported was a lightness and openness in her body.

Coach:  *When you take **decision-making** and **self-worth***
        (hands clasped together)

        ***and you separate them***
        (unclasp hands and open arms to each side),
        ***what are you NOT CREATING?***

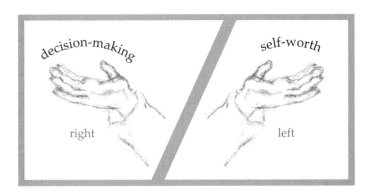

Hettie:  "Paralysis. Tightness. A static world. Frustration." She
         felt like she had permission to move.

Coach:  *When you take **decision- making** and **self-worth***
        (hands clasped together)

        ***and you separate them***
        (unclasp hands and open arms to each side),
        ***what, IF ANYTHING, are you RESISTING?***

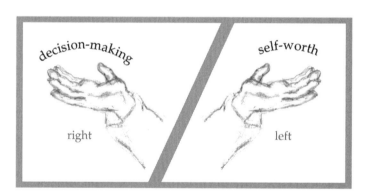

Hettie:  (pause) "Nothing."

Here is the summary of our coaching session.

**Part One**

# decision-making *EQUALS* self-worth

*What are you CREATING?*  A state of paralysis

*What are you NOT CREATING?*  Creative expression

*What are you RESISTING?*  Me... Possibilities

**Part Two**

# decision-making *DOES NOT EQUAL* self worth

*What are you CREATING?*  Space... Possibilities

*What are you NOT CREATING?*  Paralysis... Tightness

*What, if anything, are you RESISTING?*  Nothing

Hettie reported that she felt more comfortable with her hands only slightly apart. She felt timid having her hands too far apart, sensing the impact of the openness and spaciousness that she had named in the process. As we explored the space between her hands, trying on different distances, she felt the increased self-empowerment of having her arms wider and wider apart. Ultimately, she chose to embody her powerful self and to move forward both in her decision-making and in her life.

## Second Client Story

> *Through the process, Darryl understood that*
> *he had allowed himself to become a victim,*
> *playing small and hesitating to draw attention*
> *to himself.*

As a child, Darryl learned to be relatively 'invisible'. He learned that if he stayed out of the way he could be safe. As the eldest son, however, he also felt a responsibility to keep his two younger siblings safe. What he eventually fused together was the idea that, in order for him to be responsible, he had to be invisible and not stand out in any way. This was a debilitating *con-fusion* in his career as a program manager. Through the coaching conversation we explored the words he would use to summarize the dynamic. He chose *responsible* for his right hand and *invisible* for his left hand. Here is how we worked with the fusion.

**Part One**

Coach: *When you take **responsible** (right hand open)*
        *and **invisible** (left hand open)*

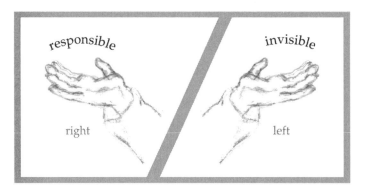

*and you put them together* (clasp hands together),
*what are you CREATING?*

Darryl:   "Chaos." He felt off center and ungrounded.

Coach:   *When you take* **responsible** (right hand open)
          *and* **invisible** (left hand open)

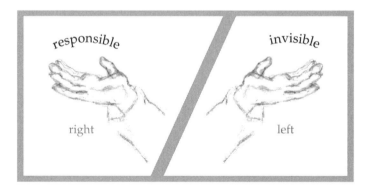

***and you put them together*** (clasp hands together),
***what are you NOT CREATING?***

Darryl: "Action." He realized that when he has the two ideas
fused together, he takes very little action.

Coach: *When you take* **responsible** (right hand open)
*and* **invisible** (left hand open)

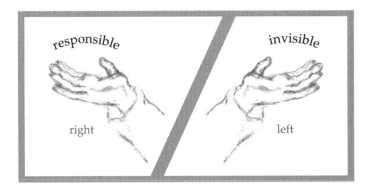

*and you put them together* (clasp hands together),
*what are you RESISTING?*

Darryl:   "Being seen." He realized that supporting his staff and
being responsible for the success of the program were
not compatible with playing small and 'being invisible'.

**Part Two**

Coach:   *When you take **responsible** and **invisible***
(hands clasped together)

*and you separate them*
(unclasp hands and open arms to each side),
*what are you CREATING?*

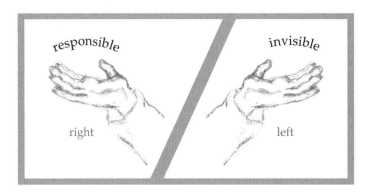

Darryl: "Me!" (Sigh!) He could breathe much easier with the
two things being separated. "I can be myself."

Coach: *When you take **responsible** and **invisible***
(hands clasped together)

*and you separate them*
(unclasp hands and open arms to each side),
*what are you NOT CREATING?*

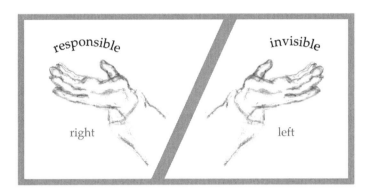

Darryl: "Being a victim." Darryl did not want to stay a victim by playing small.


Coach: *When you take **responsible** and **invisible***
(hands clasped together)

*and you separate them*
(unclasp hands and open arms to each side),
*what, IF ANYTHING, are you RESISTING?*

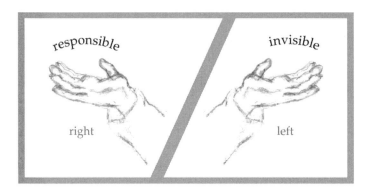

Darryl:   (pause) "Nothing." As he took a moment to check in with his body, Darryl felt relaxed and excited about the new possibilities. He felt free from some old weight.

Here is the summary of our coaching session.

**Part One**

# responsible *EQUALS* invisible

*What are you CREATING?*   Chaos

*What are you NOT CREATING?*   Action

*What are you RESISTING?*   Being seen

**Part Two**

# responsible *DOES NOT EQUAL* invisible

*What are you CREATING?*    ME

*What are you NOT CREATING?*    Being a victim

*What, if anything, are you RESISTING?*    Nothing

Once Darryl realized that he could take action, be seen and be himself, without fear of repercussions, he became very excited by the possibilities. We discussed the idea that when his habitual way of thinking and acting displayed themselves again in the future, he could clasp and unclasp his hands a few times as a way to remember his experience. The motion of separating his hands became a reminder to him to be seen and move forward.

*Con-fusions,* once realized, have the potential for clients to empower themselves. Although this practice is enhanced by doing it with the help of another person, once your clients understand the concept, they can use it on their own.

# 10 ✳ Inspired Visualization

Visualizations help your clients connect with their imaginations. They have a multitude of creative uses and can be used to assist clients to align with their hearts' desires.

For the purpose of this book, I am using what I call 'inspired visualization' as a way to momentarily suspend what the mind has made up and allow other information to come into awareness. Often something that has not previously been thought about 'comes into view'. With *inspired visualization* I am not attempting to have the client create anything per se, but rather notice what appears.

*Inspired visualizations* require clients to be sufficiently mindful to allow them to tune inward with an attitude of curiosity and non-attachment. During visualizations clients may see images, have impressions, imagine events, have sensations in their bodies, have tactile sensations, hear things, taste or smell something or access intuition.

## *Client Story*

> *In the client story below, Jen wants to be clearer about the direction her practice is moving. She continues to be mindful while reporting on what emerges.*

Coach:   (neutral, calm voice) Close your eyes and begin to turn your attention to your breathing, not trying to change anything, simply noticing your breath. (pause) Notice how your breath comes in and your breath goes out. (pause) On your next exhalation, allow more of your body weight to sink into your chair, knowing it is there to support you. (pause) Take as much time as you need.

When you are ready give me a signal and we will begin.

Jen:   (pause) Ready.

Coach:   Here you are sitting in your office five years from now. Take a moment to look around and notice your environment. When you're ready let me know what you're noticing.

Jen:   I am surrounded by soft colors... very homey... and I have a wonderful big window... I can see a beautiful big cedar outside of the window.

Coach:   And as you're looking out the window at the tree, what are you experiencing in your body?

Jen:   I feel my heart is open and my breathing is relaxed. I feel very content and satisfied.

Coach:   Keep looking around and tell me what else is there.

Jen:      I see my bookshelf lined with much-loved and much-used books. They represent all the studying and learning that I've done over the years.

Coach:   And as you take in all of your books, what do you notice in your body?

Jen:      I have a smile on my face. I am very self-satisfied.

Coach:   Feels good, huh. Is there anything else you can tell me about?

Jen:      I'm surprised at the furniture. I not only see my massage table, I also see a small circle of comfy chairs and an alcove with toys in it.

Coach:   As you get curious about the circle of chairs and the toys, what do you notice?

Jen:      (pause) Seems like there's a family environment I've created here. The chairs are for meeting with couples when discussing infertility issues. The alcove seems to be for making it possible for families to come here together. I'm not sure how that fits right now.

Coach:   You don't need to know all the answers at this point. It's enough for you to begin to picture what you may want to create in the future.

         As you are looking around your office and breathing in all that you see, you hear a knock at the door… It's your client arriving. When you're ready, get up and open the door.

Jen:     (pause) It's a young woman. She's about six months pregnant and looks absolutely radiant.

Coach:   What is she saying to you?

Jen:     She feels very grateful that not long after our acupuncture work together she became pregnant. She's here for an energy balancing treatment.

Coach:   Allow some time to take in that nourishment... Be with the satisfaction and the knowledge that you have created a joyful experience for both you and your client.

Now that Jen has had this experience, she has more to work with in relation to identifying future goals and the potential direction for her acupuncture practice. By being open to whatever showed up in her visualization, her subconscious provided her with more information.

## Embodying Animals

Another tool for making use of energy through visualization is by embodying animals. Clients may have an animal appear in a visualization or they may strongly identify with a particular animal. No matter the source, a client can embody the animal's qualities. Act it out as much as possible, either as a psychodrama or within visualization.

## Client Story

*Here is an example of working with an animal that appeared in Ed's dream.*

Ed had a horse appear in his dream. He identifies with horse energy. He saw the horse as the embodiment of both power and service. I had Ed stand up and embody the experience of standing tall and being fully alert to his surroundings. He did a combination of acting it out and being in a visualization. He then moved his body in a 'prance-like' fashion and embodied being able to move quickly and to run freely and powerfully. He saw himself galloping on the open plains.

Staying mindful, Ed identified with being in service, much like a horse serves its rider. He made the connection and understood that he could powerfully carry responsibility. He began to feel the embodiment of both power and being of service simultaneously and how it related to his current position in his company.

This is an example of coaching where a client can relate to the energy of an animal and through visualization, connect it to a life situation as a resource.

Here are some potential questions that will help clients identify the characteristics they attribute to animals and help them embody the animal.

- What is an animal that is particularly important to you? It may or may not be your favorite animal.
- What characteristics does this animal have?
- What is the animal's greatest strength?
- What attributes make this animal powerful? Free?

- What other associations or memories do you have in relation to this animal?
- What do you notice when you embody this animal?
- What do your extremities feel like? Legs? Wings?
- What's relaxing about being this animal? What's exciting about being this animal? What's challenging about being this animal?
- What do you notice when you're around a similar animal?
- What happens when you're around a variety of species?
- What's your environment like? Smells, sounds, visuals?

Visualizations can be used with clients to:

- set goals and embody how they will feel.
- embody intentions: going towards the future.
- feel the future from the present moment. Clients imagine that they have already accomplished their goal and go through the visualizations using present moment "I am…" statements as if it has already happened.
- hear what people are saying about you, or what you are saying to yourself.
- feel the emotion of attainment; embody the physical sensation of success.
- notice how success affects other parts of your life as well as other people in your life.
- speak with your future self.

Visualization in its many forms can be a powerful body-centered coaching tool.

# 11 ✸ Moving Toward Emotions

Sometimes clients come to the coaching session totally over-whelmed. The feelings are so strong it's obvious that this is the place where the coaching needs to begin. Or sometimes, strong emotions may emerge during a session. At this juncture, you may encourage clients to *move toward* the intense emotions; *move toward* them rather than move away from them.

With this technique, you assist your clients to bring their full attention to where the strong emotions are felt in their bodies. 'E-motion' is energy in motion. You are not interested in intellectual insight; you are interested in having your clients experience the energy of the sensations until they come to a place of calmness or spaciousness.

## Client Story

*This session took approximately forty minutes, which gives you an idea of the number of pauses in between dialog. It is important to listen to your own body when deciding whether to speak or to give your client more space to be with their process. For a review of sensing vs. feeling words, refer to Chapter Three, page forty-four.*

*Following is an example of a client who came to the call overwhelmed. I kept following the body sensations and continued until there was a sense of calmness or spaciousness. I gave Clint lots of time and space to be with what was happening in his body.*

Clint came to the call in the grip of strong emotions – confusion, chaos, indecision, fear. After contacting the overwhelming emotions…

Coach:   Close your eyes for a moment and notice the energy in your body as you are telling me about these emotions.

Where are you noticing the most energy in your body?

Clint:   In my stomach.

Coach:   And what's happening in your stomach?

Clint:   It's like a gigantic knot.

Coach:   Allow your awareness to go to the centre of that knot: the place where it seems the most intense.

Allow your awareness to be there fully. Notice the quality of the sensation of it.

Clint:   It's really tight.

Coach:   Just continue to notice the tightness of the knot.

Hang out there with it.

Clint:    It's uncomfortable.

Coach:    Yes, I realize that it's uncomfortable.

          What are you noticing about the knot now?

Clint:    It's eased a bit. It takes up a lot of room.

Coach:    It's big, huh.

          Allow yourself to go to the centre of that knot and put all of your awareness there.

Clint:    I feel very anxious. I don't like it here.

Coach:    Yes, you feel anxious. In life we have a natural tendency to go away from uncomfortable emotions for fear of collapsing into them.

          This time, I invite you to gently move toward it.

          I'm right here. I will hang out here with you as you're experiencing anxiety.

          What are you noticing now?

Clint:    It's lessening and my head is full of chatter and I'm having a hard time staying focused.

Coach:    Great that you noticed that. We'll go there in a minute.

          Before we do that, however, let's just check back in with the knot and see if we find anything else. Check in for a closer sense and find out if there's anything left there.

Clint:    Not much is happening. It feels like it takes up empty space.

Coach:   Is it like a spaciousness, an openness?

Clint:   No, it just feels like it occupies space and nothing is happening.

Coach:   Does it feel okay to leave that empty space for now and go to check out what's happening in your head?

Clint:   Yes.

Coach:   What are you noticing in your head now?

Clint:   It's like a constant chatter that won't leave me alone.

Coach:   Perhaps you have a metaphor for the chatter: something like 'a swarm of bees in a hive'.

Clint:   Actually, it sounds like a bunch of parrots all squawking at once. And they're really loud.

Coach:   Yeah, really loud.

Let's stay with the loud squawking parrots.

What else do you notice in your head?

Clint:   It's like my head is over-full and something is wanting to burst. Like there's not enough room.

Coach:   So what's it like when you go to the centre of all that?

Clint:   It hurts. It makes me crazy. I just want it to stop.

Coach:   Yes, I understand the urge to want to go away from the intensity of this: to distract yourself from the intensity.

Together, let's go toward the sensation and find out more about it. What's happening in your head now?

Clint: It's very constricted and it's pushing in from all sides.

Coach: Let's see if we can hang out in the centre of that.

What happens as you do that?

Clint: It's already lessened a bit and the chatter has lessened as well.

Now I can really feel a pain in my heart, in my chest.

Coach: You may want to put your hand there as we go toward it and just notice what's happening.

Clint: It's painful. It's a defeated feeling.

Coach: So as you're experiencing defeat, and your heart is hurting, what are you noticing in the most intense part of your chest?

Clint: I feel overwhelmed and I'm having trouble staying here.

Coach: Of course you are. It's no fun here.

Since this is what's happening, let's check in some more and notice the sensations.

Clint: My chest and heart are really tense.

Coach: Go to the centre of the tension and remember to stay curious.

Clint: It's lessened and now there's just a tingle.

Coach: Tell me about the tingle.

Clint: It's like a flickering flame and I'm watching it.

Coach: As you watch it, what happens?

Clint: It becomes less, like it's waving good-bye to me.

Coach: So let's keep watching it.

Clint: When I watch it, it gets smaller. When I look away it gets bigger.

Coach: I wonder if that flickering flame is what's left of the tension in your heart.

What's happening with the flame now?

Clint: I'm watching it. It's becoming less. (pause) It's gone out.

Coach: And what's there now?

Clint: Coals and embers.

Coach: What is the sensation in your body from the coals and embers?

Clint: Actually it just went to ash and now there's nothing there.

Coach: What's that like?

Clint: It's very spacious.

Coach:   Wonderful. And tell me more about "spacious".

Clint:   It's open. There's lots of space.

Coach:   And what emotion is around that spaciousness?

Clint:   I feel very calm and relaxed. There's nothing there.

Coach:   Great. Let's take a moment and really experience this spacious and calm place, really feeling grateful for it being here.

Clint:   (gives a big sigh) It feels really different now.

Coach:   Yes, it's spacious.

         Let's check in to see if there's any residue left from the overwhelming emotions.

         I want you to recall what was happening when you came to the call and see if there's anything left there when you think about the situation.

Clint:   There's nothing there now. It's all clear. Thank you.

You may have noticed that the energy moved to different places in Clint's body. Keep noticing where the energy is most intense, trusting the body to release as it moves through the process. When clients arrive at the place of calmness or spaciousness, they experience a sense of freedom; they move from being in the grip of overwhelming emotions to having choices and possibilities.

# 12 ✺ Embracing the Signal

When our body is hurting and in pain, we just want the pain and discomfort to stop. Rarely do we pause and get curious about the message that our body is sending. *Embracing the signal* is primarily an attitude. It's an attitude that says to our body, "I am listening. Thanks for signaling me to pay attention: to be mindful."

> *"Body symptoms present information of which we're unconscious. They are one of the languages the soul uses to get across to us something about itself.... We can trust the body to bring us into alignment, and we can trust the soul to speak to us through the body."*
>
> *- Gregg Levoy*
> *– Callings: Finding and Following*
> *an Authentic Life*

As an example, when you are really stressed and 'out of control', your shoulders may typically become very stiff and sore. Rather than being angry with your shoulders, another perspective could be to be thankful that they are giving you a warning signal to calm down and find a way to relax. This is a wholistic way to look after your physical and your emotional well-being.

In body-centered coaching, you become curious about physical sensations, anything from pleasure to pain. Become interested in everything that happens in the body, thereby assisting your clients do likewise.

## Client Story

*In the following client story, Cindy had the physical experience of being nauseous and as we became curious, more information became available.*

Cindy came to the call saying she woke up 'in a funk' and was feeling nauseated. She had no clear understanding of what it was about. She agreed to become curious about the sensation in her stomach that she was calling nausea.

As we became curious and quietly 'hung out' with the sensations in her stomach, a few things happened. First, she noticed that her stomach was very tight and churned up at the same time. The sensation traveled back and forth between her solar plexus and her belly. I encouraged her to increase the signal, to very slightly exaggerate the sensation. She became even more physically uncomfortable. In spite of that I encouraged her to *embrace the signal,* knowing her body was speaking somehow.

Realizing that there is always information held within body sensations, we 'stood back' and paid attention, without trying to make anything happen and without trying to make meaning of anything. Cindy was not trying to force an understanding. In this state of mindfulness, a metaphor came to Cindy – that her stomach was like a rotting, putrid kind of compost – a place where the contents were not moving through naturally and remained stuck. This increased her sense of nausea.

Continuing to pay attention to 'the compost', she allowed it just to be there, without making an effort to do anything about it. An insight 'magically' appeared. She realized that when she gets caught up in judgment, anger and making others wrong, negative energy becomes stagnant and uncomfortable within her body. She talked about a recent incident that had been making her 'want to puke' (her words) and she was feeling 'sick' about it. Her stomach had taken over her 'story'. Cindy pondered how she had 'become caught in the trap of judgment'.

She had an inner knowing, an absolute knowing, that the only way to transcend this situation was to move to an attitude of acceptance. With acceptance, she did not have to try to control anyone or anything. As we spoke about the idea of the acceptance of 'what is' without any need to control, the sensation in her stomach began to lessen. She began to breathe more fully and evenly and her whole body relaxed.

This demonstrates the importance of moving towards all of the feelings and sensations as signals and not worrying about becoming overwhelmed by them. When you pay attention to 'how you are doing' and mindfully check in with your body, it becomes easier to remain on an even keel and to move energy through your body quickly and easily. Life is about feeling things fully.

## Appreciation Story

I was at a retreat and met a young woman who was in considerable pain and could not turn her head. She had to move her whole body in order to see something beside her. Being trained in acupressure techniques, I volunteered to do a "shoulder and neck release" as a way of soothing her neck. As I was holding the acupressure points, I asked her what had happened. She told me about being out in the surf and being caught off guard by a powerful wave. Her head took the brunt of the wave, resulting in an extremely sore neck.

I commented to her, "Wow, you must really appreciate your neck." She wasn't sure how to take that comment and asked me what I meant. I said, "Well, your neck did a really good job. Sounds like the wave could have broken it. You could have been much more seriously disabled. Instead your neck held strong for you and did what it needed to do." We continued to appreciate the strength of her neck and she sent 'thank you' energy to it. Ten minutes later she got up and noticed she could turn her head from side to side and the pain had dramatically diminished. She had chosen appreciation over criticism, with amazing results.

## Giving Thanks Story

During cancer surgery, my husband Jim had six inches of his fibula bone removed from his leg so that it could be used to reconstruct his jaw. He woke up one night with excruciating pain in his leg. He was moaning and drenched in perspiration. He could not get comfortable, let alone get back to sleep. After acknowledging his pain, I said, "Maybe you need to be really thankful to your fibula for the sacrifice it made so that you could have a new jaw. How would it be to breathe in some gratitude and send it to your leg?"

As he did that, his pain began to subside and disappeared within minutes. Tears of relief ran down each of our faces. It felt like a miracle. We were both able to go back to sleep.

Your body is full of wisdom and information when you take the time to slow down and purposely listen. Your body also needs to be acknowledged and appreciated for the signals it sends.

# 13 ❋ Movement

Physically moving your body allows for shifts in your body's energy. Bodies need to move; that's their design. When you remain in one position too long, your body can start to give you signals that it's time for you to adjust your position: to stretch or to get up and move. The same applies when your mind is 'stuck' on a position for too long.

For example, when you are in a funk, you may have a certain chair that you gravitate towards; perhaps there is a particular way that you sit (rounded shoulders, head bent forward) or particular thoughts that you think (I'm such a loser).

Take a moment to become curious about where and how you do this. Experiment by finishing this sentence for yourself, "When I'm feeling down, I sometimes _____."

Next time you catch yourself in this body perspective, try standing up, looking out the window, noticing nature and all her beauty. For some, going outside for a walk is very therapeutic. You may notice that you feel differently. It doesn't mean that every trace of your mood will disappear, but it is likely that some form of movement will cause a shift. It's an intentional body perspective shift.

You can begin to 'listen' for the body position your clients are in. You can ask your clients, "What position is your body in right now?" The beauty of this question when asked over the telephone is this; because you can't physically see the position that your clients are in, as they describe it to you, they embody the position and the corresponding attitude even more. This serves to bring them into a more conscious awareness of what is happening.

As you help clients study and embody their current position, many insights and consequent learning may occur. Many habitual body and thinking patterns can come into awareness. Once the experience has been studied, invite clients to change their position. For example, have them move from sitting to standing or purposely cross the room or look out the window. Then ask, "What's different from this perspective?"

## *Body Movement Metaphors*

You may have thoughts or expressions that comment on how your clients are doing. You may say your clients are:

- moving forward in their lives.
- aware of incompletes and stepping beyond them.
- moving towards something and therefore away from something else.

You can make your own expressions physical for your clients by having their body mirror their emotional, mental, or spiritual experiences. In other words, you may think, "My client is really stepping into her or his new career." You can have the client put that into some body movement during the call. This 'stepping' movement often happens at the end of the coaching session as a way of integrating the learning.

## Client Story

*Below is an example of ending a session with having Tim use his body to step over a line. By saying 'no' to procrastination, he says 'yes' to following through.*

During this coaching session, Tim explored his habit of procrastination. He did not give himself enough time to do projects as well as he would like. Tim realized that he caused himself stress by waiting until the last minute to prepare. He had recently come very close to losing a contract that he had held for a long time. During the coaching session, Tim became aware of the damage he was doing to his career and the negative impact on his body. At the end of the coaching session, when Tim became clear about a new course of action to which he could fully commit, we decided to physicalize the process by having him actually 'step' into his new commitment to himself.

Coach:   Tim, now that you've decided on your new course of action that will work a lot better for you, I'd like you to stand up.

Tim:   Okay, I'm standing.

Coach: First, we need to find a line for you to stand at. It could be where the carpet meets the tile or it could be a design in your carpet or flooring. It could be something you place on the floor like a ruler or a piece of string. Do you see something you can use as a line?

Tim: Yes, I can use a line in the carpet.

Coach: Good. Tim, I'd like you to take this line very seriously. It represents all that we have coached about today. Please become mindful of how it feels being on the brink of making a commitment to yourself and thereby your career.

Tim: Yes, I can feel the excitement and trepidation at the same time.

Coach: Sounds like a creative place to be standing. Be sure to stay standing at this line until we design what's going to happen next.

Tim: Okay.

Coach: Standing at this line, what is behind you that you are willing to say 'no' to?

What are you stepping away from?

Tim: I'm saying 'no' to my habit of procrastination. (pause)

I'm saying 'no' to leaving things to the last minute. (pause)

I'm saying 'no' to rationalizing that I can put things off until tomorrow.

Coach:    Great. And what are you saying 'yes' to and moving towards?

Tim:      I'm saying 'yes' to diarizing in my daytimer. (pause)

          I'm saying 'yes' to following through. (pause)

          I'm saying 'yes' to being serious about what I write in my daytimer.

Coach:    Now, when you're ready, mindfully step over the line and tell me when you've done so.

Tim:      (pause) I've stepped over the line.

Coach:    What's it like on this side of the line?

Tim:      Well, there's fresh air here. I immediately noticed that the tension in my shoulders relaxed slightly. (Tim takes a big breath... a sigh.)

Coach:    Big breath. What else do you notice?

Tim:      I'm more clear-headed on this side of the line. I notice I'm standing straighter. I like it here.

Coach:    Tim, your procrastination has been a limiting habit and today is the first step in breaking that habit. Let's find a way that you can remember this side of the line. What can be a reminder for you next time you're tempted by your habit of procrastination.

Tim:      Well, I could just stand where I am now and remember. But I'm not always here in this office so I think I need something else as well.

Coach:   That makes sense to me. What is the first thing that your mind says to you when it starts to move into the habit of procrastination?

Tim:      It says, "I think I'll leave this until tomorrow."

Coach:   At this point, when you hear your self-talk, what will remind you of your decision today?

Tim:      I'll put a 'Nike' symbol on the front of my daytimer and on my desk as well. It will remind me to 'just do it'. Yeah, that will work. I like the image.

Clients often need a tangible reminder of their learning in a coaching session; an association. It could be something like:

- a picture cut out of a magazine.
- a photo.
- the words from a song written down.
- wearing a ring on a different finger, a bracelet on the other arm.
- 'post-it' notes in strategic places.
- words or images on their screen saver.
- a movement or gesture as in the *con-fusion* chapter.

The list is endless and something physical works well. Clients intuitively know what the best reminder is for them. They know what will get their attention and what won't. They are the best authority for the design of what it will be.

Body movement is a powerful resource to utilize with your coaching. It helps your clients to become grounded in their learning and it helps their bodies to remember and to integrate the learning.

# 14 ❋ Conclusion

I hope you have enjoyed both reading about and practicing the ideas and techniques contained in *Body-Centered Coaching*. The practice of body-centered coaching may be new to you. Be gentle and patient with yourself as you begin to use some of the ideas and techniques with your clients. To get started, begin by practicing with one client or with one technique at a time. As you become more comfortable and you see how you can be creative with the practice, add more to your list.

Remember that coaching is about curiosity in service to your clients' learning. Anything that is respectfully experimented with from that perspective enhances the overall energy and intention of coaching.

Remain curious, be mindful and use your empowered listening skills and begin – begin to use, create, have fun with, and experiment with the concepts in this book. Have a beginner's mind. When in doubt, ask your clients, "What needs to happen now?" It's one of my favorite questions; the client always has some idea of what needs to happen next.

# CONCLUSION

# Bibliography

## *Books*

Arbinger Institute
> Leadership and Self-Deception,
> The Arbinger Institute, Utah, 2000

Bond, Suzan
> Boost Your Intuitive Intelligence: 6 Steps to
> Understanding How Your Intuition Works, e-book,
> www.suzanbond.com, 2004

Field, James
> The Experience of the Shift to Internal Authority,
> Unpublished Doctoral Dissertation, Columbia Pacific
> University, San Rafael, 1994

Kabat-Zinn, Jon
> Full Catastrophe Living: Using the Wisdom of Your
> Body and Mind to Face Stress, Pain and Illness,
> Delta, New York, 1991

Wherever You Go There You Are: Mindfulness
Meditation in Everyday Life,
Hyperion, New York, 1994

Kurtz, Ron
Body-Centered Psychotherapy: the Hakomi Method,
LifeRhythm, Mendocino, CA, 1990

Kurtz, Ron and Prestera, Hector
The Body Reveals,
Harper and Row, San Francisco, 1976

Levoy, Gregg
Callings: Finding and Following an Authentic Life,
Three Rivers Press, New York, 1997

Martin, Donna
Remembering Wholeness: InSight Methods,
Cariboolinks Publishing, Canada, 2002
www.donnamartin.net

Tolle, Eckhart
The Power of Now: a Guide to Spiritual Enlightenment,
Namaste Publishing Inc., Vancouver, Canada, 1997

Wheatley, Margaret J.
Turning to One Another: Simple Conversations to
Restore Hope to the Future,
Berrett-Koehler Publishers, San Francisco, 2002

Wilber, Ken
No Boundary: Eastern and Western Approaches to
Personal Growth,
Shambhala, Boston, 2001

Wolinsky Stephen
    Trances People Live: Healing Approaches in Quantum
    Psychology,
    Bramble Company, Connecticut, 1991

## *Newsletters*

Badenhop, Charlie
    Pure Heart, Simple Mind
    www.seishindo.org

Field, Marlena
    Bountiful Books,
    www.BodyMindSpiritCoaching.com

Richardson, Cheryl
    Life Makeover for the Year,
    www.cherylrichardson.com

## *Audios*

McCall, Carol
    The Empowerment of Listening,
    Upline Press, Charlottesville, 1997

# BIBLIOGRAPHY

# Testimonials

"The simple and powerful wisdom in *Body-Centered Coaching* will help you access far more presence, intuition and power with your clients. It's a must read for any coach aspiring to mastery."

*- Steve Mitten, MCC*

"Sometimes, when we misplace our keys, we can't go where we want to go. When this happens we find ourselves searching frantically through the house. We might even go through our pockets or handbag over and over again looking for the missing keys. Why do we do this? Shouldn't the first time we looked have told us that the keys weren't there?

Likewise, we exhaust our minds by looking for answers that aren't really in them. Marlena Field, in her book *Body-Centered Coaching: Using The Body As A Resource For Change*, shows us how to facilitate change by using the body to find the answers that the mind needs.

*Body-Centered Coaching* is first of all a book about listening and what to listen for. Through Empowered Listening we learn to listen from an open place where our intuitive, higher self can begin to hear the dilemmas, confusions, beliefs, keywords, feelings and resources that are embedded in what our clients are telling us. From this place of Empowered Listening we can also listen to the insightful messages from our own body and learn to use them in service of our clients.

Marlena teaches us how to use mindfulness as a tool to help clients study the messages from their own bodies. We learn how to lead our clients into a place of quiet awareness where the deeper emotional messages from their bodies–the missing keys they need to get their lives moving–become available.

*Body-Centered Coaching* teaches a number of ways to help clients access the rich information that paying attention to the body brings into our session work. It is illustrated with lively client stories that bring the method to life and show us how to do it.

*Body-Centered Coaching* is a special and useful book. It condenses into a slim volume much of the wisdom of the body-centered traditions, making it easily available to coaches, counselors and body-workers."

*- Arnold W. Porter, M.Ed., RCC*


"Normally I have trouble getting past the first two chapters of a self-help book. I read *Body-Centered Coaching* in one sitting. But don't let its easy read fool you. This book is powerful. There are gold nuggets too numerous to mention. I was blown away."

*- Val Sharp, CPCC*

"Years ago I read *Lazy Man's Guide to Enlightenment*, a slim volume that was profound and easy to read at the same time. That book was a guide to Mind in a way that I've never seen since. This book will do the same for Body – a guide that is clean and elegant, at the same time both simple and profound. When a practitioner hits on a deeper truth, the result is often simple. This is that book for the body – a way of accessing and understanding the wisdom of the body. Every therapist should have this book in their toolkit. A lay person can work with this book towards a greater understanding of their own Body wisdom."

*- Jan Sommer, Ph.D.*
*Marriage and Family Therapist*

"Whether you are a seasoned coach or just entering the coaching field this book will be a most valuable resource in your business. *Body-Centered Coaching* contains valuable information on developing a positive coaching relationship using the principles collected from the fields of eastern and western approaches. Written to meet the needs of coaches at every level, this practical book takes readers through the most fundamental coaching framework to a more evolved 'mental' and 'physical' connection. By the time you finish this book you will have a completely new sense of mind and body awareness in yourself and in your clients."

*- Sherry LeBlanc, CEC CPT*
*ICF Chapter President, VI Coaches, 2004-05*

## ORDER ONLINE or BY PHONE

To order *Body-Centered Coaching* as a soft-cover book or as an e-book please visit: www.BodyMindSpiritCoaching.com

You may also order books by calling **toll free**: 1-877-778-2349.

## ABOUT THE AUTHOR

Marlena Field is a Certified Professional Co-Active Coach with training in personal and professional coaching, leadership development and entrepreneurial skills. Her background has included being a body-centered therapist, acupressure practitioner and school teacher.

## Marlena offers:

- Individual body-centered coaching.
- Group coaching.
- Supervision: for coaches and other helping professionals who want to hone their body-centered skills.
- In-person seminars based on Body-Centered Coaching.
- A variety of tele-seminars.
- Speaking engagements.

## For more information:

www.BodyMindSpiritCoaching.com
marlena@bodymindspiritcoaching.com
Toll free: 1-877-778-2349